More Praise for *This Is Day One*

"I have a problem with most leadership books. They scream from mountaintops. They quote superstars. And the authors play the role of preacher on a pedestal. But Drew Dudley is different. The pedestal has been kicked away. The superstars replaced by everyday people. And what shines through? The magical wisdom of life-changing stories on how we can be better people and live better lives. This isn't a why book. It's a *how* book. You already know leadership matters. Now here's how to do it."

—Neil Pasricha, *New York Times* bestselling author of
The Book of Awesome and *The Happiness Equation*

"*This Is Day One* is a gem of a book! Not only does Drew Dudley show us how we are all leaders in our own way, he outlines how to help ourselves and others recognize and operationalize leadership abilities. Most importantly, Dudley shows us how, in a few steps, we can make this world a much better place in which to live. *This Is Day One* is interesting, profoundly thoughtful, chock full of personal stories, and, above all, a pleasure to read. It will change you forever."

—Major General Erika Steuterman, USAF (retired)

"Drew Dudley is one of the greatest leadership experts of our time. If you care about accomplishing your goals and unleashing your fullest potential, this book is written for you. Dudley provides true stories, genuine insights, and clear strategies that will allow you to reach new levels of success and impact. Whether you're a CEO or recent graduate, you'll uncover incredible lessons that could transform your life." —Shane Feldman, CEO, Count Me In

"If you're looking for a refreshing and new take on leadership, look no further than *This Is Day One*. It provides the reader with opportunities to implement its systems in everyday situations—from your interactions with a barista at your coffee shop to a meeting with your CEO. Dudley provides the reader with easy-to-understand stories, offering us tools we can adopt immediately. I recommend this book to everyone, from those just starting out their career to those in the C-suite."

—Melody Khodaverdian, VP Partnerships, *Forbes*

"This book is a game-changer. Drew Dudley cuts through the noise and explains what leadership really should be. His thought-provoking stories and candor will change the way you view your leadership, life, career, and relationships. Whether you're leading an executive team to an IPO or an elementary school class to pursue their dreams, *This Is Day One* will guide you through a leadership framework you can use to change your life forever."

—Derrick Fung, CEO, Drop Technologies, Inc.

"A deeply personal and inspiring guide for how to live and lead in a whole-hearted way. Drew Dudley offers practical but profound advice on how to live our best lives. He speaks to the emotional courage and honesty required to live in a meaningful way and to bring out the best in others."

—Annie Simpson, Assistant Director,
Institute for Leadership Education
in Engineering, University
of Toronto

"After three decades spent in the fitness and franchise industry, I've had a courtside seat to personal leadership, and Drew Dudley has provided the blueprint in *This Is Day One*. Whether it's your business, your family, or your health, you can't lead others until you lead yourself. Start building a better life right now by reading this book on your Day One!"

—Chuck Runyon, CEO, Self-Esteem Brands:
Anytime Fitness & Waxing in the City

"Drew has a talent for making leadership accessible to everyone. His writing leaves you feeling empowered to lead in the simple moments by using personal strengths and values to navigate the spaces where you live and work. The relatable stories and insightful leadership lessons throughout *This Is Day One* make it a pleasure to read. It would be a perfect addition to any personal, educational, or organizational leadership curriculum."

—Dr. Amy C. Barnes, Senior Lecturer, Higher Education
and Student Affairs, College of Education and
Human Ecology, The Ohio State University

"*This Is Day One* focuses on the leaders within each of us and reminds us that each interaction, each accomplishment, and each day is paramount in growing as a leader, both now and in the future. Drew Dudley provides the essential steps to not bask in the virtues of a chosen few elite leaders but rather celebrate the influence and impact each person has as a leader—today! A must-read for those looking for how to lead in a way that inspires hope and change."

—Dr. Matthew Ohlson, Taylor Leadership Institute,
University of North Florida

"Your leadership journey starts here. Practical, inspiring, and raw, Drew Dudley provides honest stories and concrete mental models that are valuable for everyone. *This Is Day One* will redefine how you think about leadership and provide you with the essential tools to feel and act like a better leader—today and every day."

—Satish Kanwar, VP of Product, Shopify

"*This Is Day One* is for anyone who wants to improve their practice of leadership. Dudley is a wonderful storyteller as he walks you through a process that achieves in a book what I hope my students glean in a semester: how to be a reflective leadership practitioner. I appreciate how Dudley does not confuse leadership (the process) with leader (the person), for when we only focus on the latter we forget the most important part of the former: the others involved. Dudley is constantly reflecting on his impact on others, and I hope this book encourages others to do the same."

—Dr. Tara Widner-Edberg, Lecturer of Leadership Studies, Iowa State University

"The stories in *This Is Day One* show that leadership is a daily commitment. It's not about extraordinary accomplishments or intimidating job titles, but a consistent reinforcement of what we believe in. We need to choose to be leaders on a daily basis, every day, for the rest of our lives. Drew Dudley's own story illustrates the power of such choices, day in, day out.... *This Is Day One* will help you be principled, consistent, and surprise you with just what you're capable of."

—Wojciech Gryc, CEO, Canopy Labs

THIS IS DAY ONE

THIS IS DAY ONE

A Practical Guide to Leadership That Matters

Drew Dudley

hachette
BOOKS

NEW YORK

Hachette Go, an imprint of Hachette Books
Hachette Book Group
1290 Avenue of the Americas
New York, NY 10104
HachetteGo.com
Facebook.com/HachetteGo
Instagram.com/HachetteGo

First Trade Paperback Edition: March 2020

Hachette Books is a division of Hachette Book Group, Inc.

The Hachette Go name and logo are trademarks of Hachette Book Group, Inc.

The publisher is not responsible for websites (or their content) that are not owned by the publisher.

The Hachette Speakers Bureau provides a wide range of authors for speaking events. To find out more, go to www.hachettespeakersbureau.com or call (866) 376-6591.

Library of Congress Control Number: 2018941793

ISBNs: 978-0-316-52307-3 (hardcover), 978-0316-52299-1 (trade paperback), 978-0-316-52306-6 (ebook)

Printed in the United States of America

LSC-C

Printing 5, 2022

For Anastasia:

You made me want to build a better life for myself,
and a better self for my life.

CONTENTS

INTRODUCTION

This book examines what a leader should do on Day One. That's its only focus. It doesn't really get to day two.

This book is a leadership starter kit, so it's a book for you. Make no mistake: you're a leader. I recognize you may not think so—or may be in a leadership position you find overwhelming or wonder if you deserve—but you're a leader. Most people aren't comfortable with the title, but don't beat yourself up about it: you've been taught to feel that way. It was an untaught lesson, but untaught lessons are usually the most powerful.

I was one of the people who reinforced that lesson. For years I stood in front of university students and taught leadership theories and insights pulled from CEOs, academics, military leaders, and heads of state. Unintentionally I was building a wall between the concept of leadership and the identities of the people sitting in front of me. I was saying to them: "Leaders do big things. Leaders command lots of people. Leaders change the world."

Unfortunately, most people don't think they're doing big things. Most people don't command lots of people. Most people don't think they can change the world. As a result, most people don't think they're leaders. That's not innate—we are unconsciously *taught* that.

This book is about how you can unlearn that lesson. How you can embrace the idea that there *is* a form of leadership to which we all can and should aspire. A form of leadership you're already living without giving yourself credit for it.

Most of the leadership in your life is slipping by unrecognized and uncelebrated. It's not a character flaw or a weakness, but it's a reality. I'm going to show you how to change that.

This is the story of how leadership was redefined in my life and how it can be redefined in yours. I've filled this book with the leadership insights I've shared with hundreds of the world's most dynamic companies and prestigious schools. The Day One leadership philosophy you'll learn is the same one I've taught to hundreds of thousands of people around the globe. It's a philosophy that redefines what leadership means and who leaders truly are, and as such, it catches some people off guard.

So full disclosure: this book does not focus on how to become or be an effective manager or CEO, build high-performing teams, or acquire wealth, power, and prominence. At least not directly. It focuses on what must come before that. Acquiring positions and titles takes a number of days. This book is about one day: Day One.

Repeat Day One enough times, and the rewards you seek will come. Treat today as Day One on a march toward something better in your life, then treat tomorrow the same way. Repeat.

Many of the things that we've been taught define a leader— respect, prestige, influence, financial and social rewards— become more likely if you follow the process laid out in this book. Respect, prestige, influence, financial and social rewards are the natural *by-products* that emerge from embodying the type of leadership discussed in this book.

No, this book is not about how to become a CEO, manager, team leader, or world changer. It's a book about how to be the *type of person* who is *great* at those things.

It's about what you do on Day One, and today is Day One.

Let's get started.

PART I

This Is Day One

ONE

This Is Day One

I've had a lot of Day Ones in my life.

I've had Day One of a life without alcohol. I am powerless over alcohol, and for more than two decades it often turned me into far less than the man I want to be.

I've had Day One of being a vocal advocate for mental health awareness. Doing so has meant being open about my bipolar disorder in a world where mental illness is often confused with mental weakness. When your career relies entirely on the perceived credibility of your ideas, that can be terrifying.

I've had Day One of my life as an entrepreneur. A friend of mine once told me that "the three most addictive things on the planet are crack, carbohydrates,...and a salary." I didn't fully grasp the truth of that statement until it came time to give up a steady paycheck from a prestigious university. I wasn't sure I'd be able to feed myself, let alone build a thriving business and write a book.

I've had Day One on a weight-loss voyage of over 100 pounds. When I delivered the TEDx Talk that truly launched my career, I tipped the scales at over 300 pounds. Today, physical fitness is a huge part of my life and I no longer need to look at the scale to know when I'm healthy.

Each of my journeys—to sobriety, mental and physical health, and business success—began with a Day One. There is nothing you want to achieve "one day" that doesn't begin with a Day One. Day One is when you begin the consistent behaviors that lead to what you're hoping for one day: the weight loss, the corner office, your own business, and most importantly, feelings of satisfaction, pride, and peace.

There are going to be a lot of difficult days on your journey to recognizing and applying your leadership, so here's a fundamental premise of this book: you must treat every single one of those days like it's Day One of your journey. This idea is not unique to this book: the concept is foundational in most addiction recovery programs, is a mindset adopted by elite athletes, and is a key business philosophy of some of the world's biggest companies. This book applies the approach in a very specific context: personal leadership development.

Day Ones provide a sense of renewal, commitment, and forgiveness. When I committed to sobriety I learned that I need to treat every day of the rest of my life as if it was the first day of my recovery. My sobriety hinges on a single, non-negotiable daily behavior: choosing not to have a drink *today*. When I wake up in the morning, five straight years of making that choice doesn't matter: I must commit to it again today if I'm to be the person I want to be. All that matters are the actions of today.

If I fail (and yes, I have failed some days), I cannot consider the failure permanent. I treat the next day as another Day One: a renewal of my commitment to the behaviors that make me someone of whom I'm proud.

Living Day One leadership means embracing the same philosophy: if you want to be a leader, choose to be a leader today. Repeat that choice every day. It doesn't matter if you failed to do it yesterday or if you've done it every day for a decade: every new day begins with a recommitment to that choice.

How do you choose to be a leader? You make that choice with your actions—the behaviors you make nonnegotiable each day. This book will help you choose the right behaviors *for you*: the ones that will make you feel and act like a leader. They will be unique to you because they are intended to narrow the gap between the person you want to be and how you actually behave each day. Only you can truly know the nature of that gap, so there isn't a one-size-fits-all approach. We're going to customize it for your needs.

Working to close that gap is leadership: the leadership to which we all can and should aspire. It's the leadership I want you to acknowledge and to which I want you to commit by implementing the process in this book.

Let go of the connections in your mind between leadership and titles, money, influence, and prestige. Those things come from others and are outside of your control. Only your behaviors are within your control and the biggest determinant of how others feel about you and how you feel about yourself is *how you behave on a day-to-day basis*. Leadership isn't in the big things—leadership is in the consistent things. Develop a relentless commitment to specific daily leadership behaviors and you're living life as a leader.

Live today like a leader would on Day One and you're a leader today. Live each day this week like a leader would on Day One, you've lived a week as a leader. Live each day this month like a leader would on Day One, you've lived a month as a leader. Then a year. Then five years. Then a lifetime.

The key is to stop worrying about the weeks and years: your commitment to leadership shouldn't be over a block of time. Your commitment should be to act as a leader for a single day: Day One. Then treat every day as if it's Day One: with a renewed commitment to your most important leadership behaviors. What's possible in your life and career will grow with each subsequent version of Day One, but what's essential (those key leadership behaviors) will always stay the same.

Let's get started on exploring what your Day One might look like.

TWO

The New Guy

You won't hear from a lot of CEOs in this book. In fact, you won't hear from a lot of people who would traditionally be given the title of "leader."

That's a conscious decision. Highlighting people in a leadership book creates an implicit indication their leadership should be emulated. However, I wrote this book to show you how to better live *your* leadership, not someone else's. You may not be a senior executive, high-profile athlete, or influential politician but you *are* a leader. If you're not consciously acknowledging or engaging your leadership each day, I hope to change that.

The leadership you put into the world won't necessarily be the same as anyone else's. It may differ greatly from the type you've seen celebrated or from the leadership you've chased your whole life. That might push you to dismiss or marginalize your personal leadership, and I want to make sure you embrace it.

I don't know the nature of your leadership, but I do know it's there. It may be different than the leaders about whom you've been taught, but it's no less essential to the organizations and communities of which you are a part. I want you to hear the ideas of leaders to whom you relate and who represent your leadership reality, so there are a lot of different leadership voices in these pages.

As I chose the leadership examples for this book, I imagined a world where all money, jobs, titles, fame, influence, and our memories of who held them had been stripped away: a Day One where leaders were judged only by what they choose to do each day to positively impact themselves and others. I thought about a world where ideas and insights were validated by how useful they were, not by the title or bank account of the person delivering them. In a world like that, leaders may look a lot different than we're used to. This book features those leaders and their ideas. It has to—it was one of those leaders who provided the title.

Mustafa

I met Mustafa at dawn on the outskirts of Doha, Qatar. It was my only day off on a speaking tour of the Middle East and I was heading out "dune bashing." It had been described to me as "flying off sand mountains at 70 miles an hour." I had to try it.

I walked bleary-eyed through the front doors of my hotel to see an incredible sunrise over the desert. Leaping from a nearby 4×4 was a beaming man who bounded around the front of the vehicle, threw his arms wide and, smiling broadly, bellowed:

"Mr. Dudley! Welcome! Welcome to Mustafa's grand adventure!"

He brought his arms in to his chest and announced proudly, "I...am Mustafa!"

Everyone should introduce themselves with that kind of enthusiasm: it raises the energy of everyone around you. Unfortunately, my jet lag and lack of sleep led to the delivery of what I understand—in retrospect—was a profoundly inappropriate response. I grinned, threw my own arms wide, and bellowed, from the very bottom of my chest, my personal rendition of the Zulu cry that opens *The Lion King*:

"Nants ingonyama bagithi Baba!"

Mustafa's smile disappeared instantly. His brow furrowed. His eyes grew hard.

"That," he hissed through clenched teeth, "was MUFASA."

He opened the door to the 4×4 with a violent jerk.

"Get in!" he demanded coldly.

Concerned that I had clearly made it far less likely this man would put his full heart into returning me home in one piece, I began to back toward the hotel entrance.

"Oh...well, perhaps it's best if I don't...," I began.

Mustafa's face split into a wide smile, and he let loose with a tremendous laugh.

"Mr. Dudley! No! I am just teasing you, my friend!" He said, clearly pleased with how uncomfortable he had made me. "You are very funny! Yes, it is like *The Lion King*, but not quite! Much like you Canadians are like Americans, but not quite, right?"

He stared at me expectantly.

"Um...well," I began, not sure how to respond to that

analysis. "I wouldn't put it that way...there are a lot of subtle but important differences."

I trailed off, thrown completely off balance by my obviously mischievous guide. How did he even know that I was Canadian?

Again, Mustafa laughed uproariously and gestured to the open passenger door.

"Well then," he said happily, "you must teach me! Let us go, I am very excited!"

I climbed into the passenger seat and we were off. And my friends, he was not kidding about being excited: Mustafa vibrated with energy.

As soon as we pulled out, he began to talk, excitedly chatting about what we were about to "learn from the desert" and firing facts and stats about Canada at me (he had been told the night before I was Canadian and had done a little Internet research ahead of time). Stories about his youth, philosophies on life, the things he liked the most about Qatar, and, of course, jokes, jokes, and more jokes—it was a nonstop stream of exuberant chatter for over an hour.

It was when we started heading for the first dunes—100-foot mountains of sand emerging from the desert—that he took it to a new level. He was quite simply cackling with laughter and excitement as he pushed the accelerator toward the floor. We were absolutely flying toward what appeared to me to be a sheer drop and Mustafa was having the time of his life.

Bracing myself against the dash, I looked over at Mustafa and shouted: "Mustafa! You're having a better time than I am! You do this every day! How do you stay so excited about it?"

Mustafa looked over at me, and with a smile that showed every one of his teeth, bellowed back:

"Oh! It's my first day!"

I just about crawled out the back window.

Look, I understand that everyone has to start somewhere, but if your job involves driving me off of sand cliffs (hell, if your job involves driving me off of any cliffs really), I'd really prefer not to be assigned the new guy.

I'm going to assume that thought showed very clearly in my expression because Mustafa let out a laugh and hit the brakes. The 4×4 skidded to a halt maybe twenty feet from the edge of the dune.

At that point I had both feet on the dash and had pushed myself basically up to the roof. Mustafa put the vehicle in park and looked at me with pure amusement.

"Mr. Dudley," he began, leaning in. "Don't you realize? You *want* the new guy!"

My heart still in my throat, I managed a weak, "I'm not so sure, my friend."

"Think about it, Mr. Dudley," Mustafa replied. "Think about your first day of work! On your first day of work you show up early; you dress your best; you try everything you can to impress your boss. You are patient with your coworkers, even the ones you know right away you're not going to like. You ask all the questions you have because there's no shame in doing that when you're new. You double-check everything that you do. You stay late. You are never more committed to your job than you are on your first day. You are never more convinced it is going to be the best job you have ever had than you are on your first day."

He leaned closer and continued, "As soon as your second day of work begins, all of that starts to stop being quite so true, doesn't it?"

He leaned back with a broad smile.

"The first day that I ever came to work at this job was seventeen years ago, Mr. Dudley. But I had such an incredible experience that I promised myself something. I promised myself that I would NEVER have a second day of work."

He paused to look me right in the eye.

"Mr. Dudley, it has been my first day of work for seventeen years. Five years ago I bought this company. All I ask of anyone who works for me is that they treat every day they come to work like it is their first day. The customers love it. It's why we are the best tour company in the country."

Live every day like it's Day One. It's a concept that changed how I view leadership. I hope it will do the same for you.

THREE

Are You a Leader?

"How many of you are completely comfortable calling yourself a leader?"

I estimate I've asked that question to over a thousand audiences in the past ten years. They've represented a wide range of backgrounds and industries: CEOs, doctors, teachers, emergency responders, customer service staff, students, and professors to name just a few. They've ranged in size from groups of ten to more than ten thousand. In fact, I estimate I've asked over a quarter of a million people on five continents to ponder that question for me.

You want to know how often more than half the people in any given room have raised their hands? Less than 1 percent of the time. Once every hundred audiences or so are there more than a handful of people in a room willing to say: "I am a leader."

That's a driving force behind this book. I've studied

leadership my entire adult life and I honestly believe there is no shortage of leadership on this planet. However, we are systematically ignoring a huge percentage of the leadership that surrounds us each day—in our own lives and the lives of those with whom we interact—because we've chosen to define leadership too narrowly. This book will give you a road map for how to start changing that for yourself and the people you care about.

The older we get, the more we treat the term "leader" like it's something we require *permission* to use: we hope that *one day* the money we make and our professional achievements will be enough for some external group or individual to bestow some title, credential, accolade, or degree we believe we need to deserve to call ourselves a "leader."

We celebrate that permission once we receive it. We *want* people to know when we've "earned" the permission to lead. In fact, we advertise it on email signatures, LinkedIn profiles, and business cards. I've learned that until people have been given that external permission to position themselves as a leader, they fear that claiming the title for themselves (especially in front of other people) will demonstrate a level of cockiness and arrogance with which they don't wish to be associated.

This is part of a society-wide tendency to make leadership into something bigger than us and something beyond us. The perception is that leadership is determined by money, titles, and influence, and therefore reserved for a relatively small subsection of the population. After a couple of decades in the world of higher education, I believe how we teach leadership plays a huge role in that perception.

Think about how you learned what a "leader" was. My

guess is you were given examples to illustrate the concept, and I'm betting those examples were giants. They were presidents, scientific groundbreakers, titans of business, and conquerors of nations. I'm betting the vast majority were also white men. Young people today are being given the same sort of examples. We tell them, "Look at Warren Buffett invest! Look at Steve Jobs innovate! Look at Mark Zuckerberg build an online empire!"

As for our daughters and granddaughters—if you want a glimpse into the lessons they're learning about what leaders look like, do a Google image search of the word "leader." My first search revealed a penguin, a chicken, and two different types of fish portrayed as a leader before the first image of a woman appeared.

I shared that fact with an audience just a couple of years ago. Afterward a woman approached me to say: "Do me a favor, go home tonight and do a Google image search for the term 'CEO.'"

The top search result? A photo of the "CEO Barbie" doll, complete with cell phone, laptop, and skirt that only the most generous among us would call "mid-thigh." That image is problematic in more ways than I can list here, but I will point out three.

1. It is representative of the fundamental, systemic barriers to leadership that exist for most people who don't look like…well…me.
2. When audiences are presented with that search result, most people laugh. It's not funny.
3. Barbie is a giant in our culture.

A consequence of using giants (notably straight, white, male giants) as the primary examples of leadership is that most of us begin to devalue the leadership that *we* demonstrate every day. We start to let moments when we embody leadership pass by without allowing ourselves to take credit for them or feel good about them. The problem is, for better or for worse, the things that make us feel good are the things that we find ourselves driven to do on a daily basis. When people around us demonstrate leadership and we fail to publicly recognize those moments *as* leadership, we're making it less likely they'll be repeated. When we fail to recognize the leadership that surrounds us, we effectively erase it from our organizations, our communities, and our lives. Most of the leadership on the planet is going unnoticed and uncelebrated—yours included.

And we need it. We need more hands to go up. We need janitors making minimum wage to recognize they have as much right to raise their hand and call themselves a leader as the CEO of a Fortune 500 company. We need to teach our kids that money, titles, power, and influence aren't appropriate criteria for identifying leaders because they exclude the vast majority of the people on the planet. We need them to know *now* so they don't take the same thirty years I did to figure it out.

When I graduated high school in the spring of 1996, I thought that I was everything a student was supposed to be because I had done everything I had been *told* to do: I graduated with an A+ average as the valedictorian, prom king, and one of the captains of the football team. In my "spare time," I was one of the editors of the school paper and president of the Student Union (because only in high school can you control the government and the press at the same time and no one has a problem with it).

Everything I did was about looking good on paper. A very specific piece of paper: my résumé. My entire life was about filling up that double-sided sheet of paper. On it went my grades, my extracurriculars, and all my volunteer work, awards, and accolades. I evaluated everything I did based on how good it would look on that single sheet: the better I looked on paper, the more likely I'd get into a "good" school. The better the school I attended, the better my résumé would look to potential employers. My whole life was about impressing people I hadn't met yet: admissions counselors I hadn't met yet, bosses I hadn't met yet, potential future spouses I hadn't met yet. It was all aimed at helping me become one of the select few: outperform everyone, collect the highest numbers on the top right-hand corner of my tests and assignments—the most letters after my name—and one day I would earn the right to be in that special, tiny subsection of society who got to call themselves "leaders."

Getting into that tiny percentage was my mission in life, until a single interaction messed with my perception of what "leadership" was all about, made me realize our lives should not be lived for people we haven't yet met, and started the shift that led to this book.

The Lollipop Moment

In October of 2002, I was twenty-five years old, a year and a half removed from earning my bachelor's degree and still living in the same small university town where I'd been for almost six years.

Your mid-twenties is the new puberty—full of big changes, plenty of angst, and more than its fair share of confusion and self-doubt. A few less hormonal changes than the original puberty, a whole lot more debt, and for a lot of people about the same amount of living with your parents.

I wasn't sure what was next in my life, but faced with moving back in with Mom and Dad, I figured it was a heck of a lot more appealing to stick around a place where I had keys to the bar. I was comfortable, accomplished, and well known around campus—a big fish in a small pond. I'd graduated with first-class honors and figured I'd eventually get around to grad school and more letters after my name, which of course would eventually lead to impressive titles, a big staff, and more dollars in my bank account. That's how life worked in my mind: if you wanted to be rewarded, you figured out what the person at the front of the room wanted (be it a teacher, professor, or boss) and delivered it to them better than the person next to you.

Then a tornado landed on my parents' house while they were in it. They survived but my childhood home was flattened. Mom and Dad were homeless, and with my sister on the west coast and me on the east, dealing with it all alone. It was literally an act of God indicating it was time for me to leave the bubble of university and face the real world. A good-bye party was organized at the bar I'd helped run and plans for your standard "last night before becoming a grown-up" festivities ensued.

Early in the party, I was approached by a young woman I'd seen around campus but had not to my knowledge ever spoken with.

"Hi, Drew," she said.

"Hey!" I said with that *"so good to see you even though I have no idea who you are"* enthusiasm.

She laughed.

"It's all right. I know you don't know who I am, but I remember the first time I ever met you."

She continued: "I got here four years ago. And the night before my first day I was in a hotel room with my mom and dad. I don't know why, but for some reason that night I completely freaked out. I was utterly and totally convinced I wasn't ready for this; that I was going to fail miserably and humiliate myself and my parents. I was such a basket case that I actually broke down crying."

She smiled. "But my parents were totally amazing. They told me, 'Look, we know you're scared. Trust us, we are way more scared than you are. But you've worked so hard for this—you owe it to yourself to go tomorrow and see what it's like. So, here's the deal: we go to registration tomorrow, and if at any point during the day you really feel like you just can't do it, tell us and we'll take you home. We're going to love you no matter what. But if you don't at least try tomorrow, we think you'll end up regretting it for a long time, and it's our job to make sure you don't do things like that.

"You know what?" she continued. "Looking back on it now, I realize that I had no idea what I was going to do with my life, but I had never actually been presented with an option that didn't include going to university. All I'd ever been taught was that it was basically mandatory if you didn't want to end up in a crap job, so I knew they were right.

"So, I came here on the first day and got into line. And everybody was yelling. Seriously, everyone was in matching shirts and face paint and doing these coordinated cheers. And I know that they were just trying to make us feel welcome, and I know that works if you're an extrovert, but if you're an introvert that scares the crap out of you."

We laughed, and she went on.

"Anyway, I'm standing there on my first day, completely overwhelmed by all this noise, and I said to myself, 'This is another place where only extroverts are valued. I'm not going to spend four years of my life where you have to yell to fit in.'

"And I quit. At least in my mind I did. Standing there in line on my first day I just decided I was done. The funny thing is as soon as I made that decision it was like this incredible feeling of peace came over me. I just knew somehow that it was the right decision for me.

"So, I turned to my mom and dad to tell them to take me home like they said they would, but before I could say anything, you came out of the nearest building wearing the stupidest hat I've ever seen a man wear before."

(I regularly thank God that camera phones are a product of the new millennium.)

She smiled at the memory.

"You had this big sign around your neck that said, 'Students Fighting Cystic Fibrosis' and a bucket full of lollipops. You were walking along the lineup of all of us first years and our parents making jokes, talking about your charity and trying to convince us to get up early on Saturday to come and shine shoes all day as a fund-raiser.

"But then you got to me…and you just stared at me," she

said, playing the role of me in the story and locking eyes for a long, silent moment.

"It was creepy."

I laughed nervously, not sure where she was going with all of this.

"But then you turned to the guy next to me and you smiled. You reached into your bucket, took a lollipop, and held it out to him, saying, 'Dude—you're going to be stuck in this line for another two hours. The woman next to you is absolutely beautiful. Break the ice, big guy. Give her this lollipop."

She demonstrated how I'd apparently done this by shoving an imaginary lollipop in my face.

"You know what?" she continued. "I'd never seen this guy before in my life, but I've still never seen anyone get so embarrassed. He wouldn't even look at me, just stuck the lollipop in my general direction and stared straight ahead.

"Well, I felt so bad for this guy because it was his first day too and now everyone was staring at him. So, I took the lollipop just to let him off the hook.

"As soon as I did, your entire demeanor changed. All of a sudden, you looked incredibly disappointed, upset even.

"You turned to my parents, and in a really loud voice so that everyone could hear, said: 'Look at your little girl! Just look at her! It is her first day away from home—her first day without mom and dad to hold her hand... *and already she's taking candy from a stranger!*'

"Well," she said. "Everybody lost it. For like twenty feet in every direction absolutely everyone started howling."

She smiled and shook her head before continuing.

"Look, I know this sounds cheesy, but in that moment when everyone was laughing, something changed in me. Something in my head said, 'Don't quit today...you can quit tomorrow, but don't quit today.'

"You know what?" she said softly, looking away from me, "I never did. I graduate in a few weeks."

She turned back to me.

"I've seen you around campus, but I haven't spoken to you once in the four years since that happened. But I heard that you were leaving, and I knew that before that happened, I had to come here and tell you something."

She paused, as if considering what to say next.

Finally, she said, "Drew, you've been an incredibly important person in my life and I never said thank you for it. I need to do that now and tell you I wish you nothing but the best. Good luck, okay?"

And she walked off.

I had no idea what to say. I was completely flattened by the story and just stood there, staring at her departing back.

After a few steps, she glanced back, realized the state in which she had left me, and with an amused expression, walked back over.

"Well," she said. "There is one more thing you probably should know."

She paused, smiling.

"I've been dating that guy for four years since you introduced us in line that morning."

A year and a half later, after I had moved a thousand miles away, a wedding invitation arrived. She married the dude.

And you know what?

I have *absolutely no recollection of that moment.*

That moment may have been the greatest moment of leadership in my life. It perhaps represented the most significant impact I'd ever had on another human being. It was powerful enough to cause a woman to walk up to a complete stranger and say, "You have been an incredibly important person in my life," and yet I didn't even remember it.

At that point I had spent the better part of my life trying to achieve goals that would impress others in the hopes it would earn me an opportunity to have an impact on the world. In that moment I was reminded that our leadership is not demonstrated by the goals we achieve but in how we behave in the pursuit of those goals.

The charity campaign I was promoting that day went on to set a new fund-raising record. The day the numbers came in I was celebrated as a leader. I had consciously worked for four months to matter on that single day, yet I had made a far more significant impact in a single unplanned moment that I didn't even remember. In the four months I had worked for that single accomplishment, 120 days had passed. Any impact I made on any given one of them was purely coincidental: I wasn't consciously trying to live as a leader *each day*—I was trying to look like a leader *one day*.

I wasn't yet treating leadership as a daily practice. I wasn't yet living each day like it was Day One. That shift is necessary before you can begin to see real momentum in your leadership journey.

Everyday Leadership

Most people do not evaluate their leadership day to day, they do so over periods of time: a semester, a fiscal quarter, a year, five years. We evaluate our leadership based on how well our plans are turning out: *I planned to be married by twenty-eight and have one child, to be making $100,000 a year and on the fast track to partner. I'm behind on those goals, so I obviously don't have my act together. How can I lead anyone else, if I can't reach my own goals?*

Don't get me wrong, it's important to have plans. I've always loved the adage *"Dreams don't come true. Goals come true. A goal without a plan is just a dream."*

It's important to have goals and plans to reach them. Just ensure you never lose sight of the fact that your most enduring legacy will very likely have nothing to do with your plans. The greatest impact you will have on the people around you and the organizations of which you are a part *will almost always be a result of the unplanned consequences of your everyday actions.*

When we evaluate ourselves as people and leaders, however, the focus rarely falls on the ordinary days. Instead our attention turns to the "extraordinary" days in our lives: days when things happen that don't usually happen.

Yes, there are extraordinary days in our lives, both positive and negative. Positive extraordinary days feature promotions, the achievement of major goals, and overcoming major obstacles. On negative extraordinary days, we fail as an individual or as a team, are denied something we truly feel that we deserve, and hurt (or are hurt by) people about whom we truly care. We can learn a lot about ourselves and about our organizations on these extraordinary days. However, never forget that the extraordinary days in our lives are always outnumbered by the ordinary days when we live our lives and contribute to our work without tremendous fanfare.

The nature and frequency of our extraordinary days are

determined by how we behave on our ordinary days. Long-term success or failure is fostered in our ordinary days. Our true character, and that of our teams, is revealed by how we behave in our ordinary days.

Why then, when we evaluate our lives, do we focus on the relatively small percentage of "extraordinary days"? Part of the answer lies in the fact that most of us traveled through an education system in which we went to class for twelve weeks but our final grade was often determined by how we performed on three days: a couple of midterms and a final. The day-to-day work you put into attending class, studying, and writing assignments wasn't what mattered: just three big, important days. It's a perspective on life I don't think wears off as we get older: *what matters is how you step up on the big days—on the days when the spotlight shines and the "chips are on the table."* This perspective diminishes the importance of most days to most people, making it less likely that we feel a sense of urgency to seize each day as an opportunity for leadership.

Instead we keep count of our extraordinary days and try to close the gap between how many extraordinary days we've had and how many we feel we need to really "matter" in this world. In our minds closing that gap requires big things: promotions, athletic accomplishments, a wedding, the birth of a child. We believe it's the big things in our lives that move us toward the point where we matter, and big things happen over time. Focusing on the simple, everyday things isn't going to close that gap.

But simple doesn't mean little. Simple, consistent, impactful behaviors are what generate the momentum needed to accomplish the most significant things in our lives. Perhaps more importantly, simple impactful behaviors can provide us with daily evidence that we matter. We need that evidence daily—not just a few times a year. It's available to us every day, but as you'll see in the next chapter, far too few people are taking advantage of that.

FOUR

Plan to Matter

Why do you matter?

Seriously. Take a moment, put the book down, and articulate your answer to that question out loud. At some point during most of my presentations, I will point at someone in the audience and ask that question. The reaction is pretty consistent: somewhere between utter confusion and sheer terror.

If you have kids, take a moment and ask them that question. If they have not yet gone to school, my guess is that they will give you a heart-melting response. Once we send them to school, however, they very quickly come to believe that why they matter is no longer up to them to determine—it's supposed to be evaluated by someone else. Unfortunately, that's not a lesson we unlearn as we grow older.

The first time I asked this question, it was to a remarkable student right before he graduated, and he responded, "I *don't* matter yet. That's why I'm working so hard." I couldn't believe it. This young man had been a tremendous force for positive change at our university and had touched the lives of many people, including mine, but he didn't feel that he mattered? I asked a few other students. More of the same.

"Oh God, I don't know."
"I guess because I try to make a difference?"
"That's a stupid question, leave me alone, I have to study."

I was fascinated. I added the question to my presentations and interviews. I've asked CEOs, entrepreneurs, teachers, doctors, lawyers, and really anyone I could get to listen. I've asked hundreds of people "Why do you matter?" and many of them have been, by every objective measure, wildly successful. They've run companies, made millions, fought for justice, and saved lives.

Yet 90 percent of the people I ask either cannot answer the question or offer a halfhearted response they clearly just cooked up. As someone who spent fifteen years in higher education I had to ask myself: *How can we call what we are providing an education when some of the most intelligent, dynamic, passionate, caring, compassionate, and well-educated people on the planet cannot answer the question "Why do you matter?" because no one has ever asked them before?*

Why do so many extraordinary people struggle with that question? It's because we *hope* to matter. We *hope* to lead. We *hope* to make a difference. Look, hope is a wildly powerful force—and we should foster hope in our lives and in the lives of everyone we touch—but hope is a lousy strategy. If you want to matter, you must plan to matter. You must plan to lead. You must plan to make a difference.

Day One is about making those plans.

Your Personal Leadership Philosophy

Planning to matter starts with this question: *What is your personal leadership philosophy?*

A personal leadership philosophy is a set of beliefs and principles you use to evaluate information and respond to people and situations. An effective personal leadership philosophy allows anyone who hears it to gain an understanding of your values, priorities, approach to decision making, and what you expect from yourself and others.

If you can't tell me your personal leadership philosophy in under thirty seconds; if you can but it's the first time you've articulated it out loud in the past three days; or if someone who works with you closely cannot tell me your personal leadership philosophy—you don't actually have one. At least not one that is truly impacting the way you behave.

It's difficult sometimes to reflect on macro-level questions like this one, but developing an answer is crucial. Here's why:

- Individuals able to articulate a personal leadership philosophy score over 110 percent higher on overall leadership effectiveness than those who cannot.
- Those who work with leaders who have a clear leadership philosophy evaluate their leaders as 140 percent more effective than those who work with leaders who lack a clear philosophy

- People who work with leaders who have a clear personal leadership philosophy report higher levels of:
  - Team spirit
  - Pride in their organization
  - Commitment to their organization's success
  - A willingness to work hard to meet the organization's objectives
  - Trust
- Leaders who have a clear leadership philosophy score 135 percent higher on measures of trust than those who do not.[1]

A personal leadership philosophy isn't just a "nice thing to have"; research has proven that it makes you impact others in a more positive way. If you don't have a personal leadership philosophy, you don't have a plan for leading every day: you're hoping to lead, you're not planning to lead.

This book is about a personal leadership philosophy: This is Day One. The Day One leadership philosophy represents a daily commitment to making decisions and engaging in behaviors that are consistent with your core leadership values.

If you feel you already have a personal leadership philosophy, that's totally fine. It's not an either–or proposition and most philosophies supplement and reinforce one another well. The Day One philosophy will almost certainly help you apply your current leadership philosophy more consciously and consistently.

In fact, I incorporated my previous leadership philosophy seamlessly into the This is Day One approach. For many years,

I relied on this philosophy: *When you don't know what to do in a situation, ask yourself: "What would the person who I want to be do in this situation?" Then do that.*

Simple? Yes. Easy to follow? Hell no.

Very few people have given a significant amount of thought to who it is they really want to be. Most want to be fundamentally "good" as opposed to "bad," but I've found that relatively few have taken the time to get much more specific than that.

Perhaps that's because when we're young we're judged and graded on what others expect us to know. We get used to the big questions in our lives coming from *other* people and we learn to pay closest attention to the things on which we will be tested. Those tests rarely feature questions about who we want to be, how we understand our core values, and which criteria we should use to make difficult decisions. As a result, many of us become our own worst subject. We grow up being asked what we want to *do* when we grow up, not who we want to *be*. The former means meeting the expectations of others, the latter asking tough questions of ourselves. We're not forced to ask those tough questions and answering them can be uncomfortable, so many of us choose not to.

I was one of those people who chose not to ask myself those tough, uncomfortable questions, and on Day One in front of a classroom an eighteen-year-old student showed me why that was a problem.

"Could You Explain What That Word Means?"

I was twenty-eight years old the first time I stood in front of a group of university students. It was a workshop on leadership theory with a heavy focus on transformational and servant leadership. Trying to make the content a little more relatable (I've often said "theory" is the word you add to interesting things to make them boring), I spent the last half hour covering some of the ideas presented in this book, namely, that there is a form of leadership of which all of us are capable. At the close of the workshop, a young woman approached with a comment few educators enjoy hearing at the end of their first day in the classroom.

"Sir," she said shyly, "I don't get it."

"What exactly is it you don't understand?" I asked.

"I don't think I understand leadership anymore sir."

"Well," I said with a small smile, "I wouldn't worry too much about that—we have all semester to explore what leadership means."

She shook her head. "That's just it. I understood leadership before I came today. Now I'm afraid I don't."

I've come to hope that many people walk out of my workshops feeling this way, but back on my first day, I felt I had let this young woman down.

"What do you mean?" I asked.

"Well," she said. "I'm studying abroad here, and in my country, we're told that the smartest people make the best leaders. I was always taught the smartest people are the ones who get the best grades. If you get good grades it's your way of showing the world that one day you deserve to be a leader. If you don't, it's your way of demonstrating you never deserve that responsibility.

"But," she continued, "what you talked about today makes

me think that leadership means something different in Canadian."

I suppressed a chuckle at the suggestion "Canadian" is a language before she added: "Can you explain to me what 'leadership' means in simple English?"

I smiled confidently and opened my mouth to provide my well-rehearsed and carefully considered personal definition of leadership—a definition I'm sure she (and I) expected to be brilliant. However, nothing came out. My mind was blank. Not only did I lack a sophisticated answer to her question, I lacked any answer at all. I knew the theories of leadership— how it had been studied, explained, and understood throughout history—and I could help people identify and develop the skills that were integral to leadership. What I didn't have was my own explanation of what leadership meant, "in simple English."

I was facing one of those questions to which you're certain you have the answer until someone actually asks you the question. I was genuinely shaken by the realization that while I recognized many of the values I hoped to embody in my life, I hadn't taken the time to define them.

The problem is this: *If you don't take the time to define the things that you hope will define you, you're always going to feel as if you aren't living up to the person you want to be.*

How do you give yourself credit for hitting a target you've never actually identified? If you don't clearly define what "leadership," "respect," or "accountability" mean to you, if you don't turn them into specific goals so you *know* when you've hit them, you may be (and probably are) embodying those values every single day but never giving yourself the opportunity to acknowledge that fact. Moments where you're living up to your core values are slipping by uncelebrated.

The celebrations in our lives and work give us momentum, push us forward, and give us the strength we need to get through difficult times. Celebrations are an essential part of life and leadership, and setting goals is basically planning celebrations. You set goals you want to reach in your career, your financial life, and your health and fitness. Personal leadership is about spending just as much time—and investing just as many resources—in setting and pursuing goals *for your character* on a daily basis. This starts with being able to identify and define the core values you hope will drive you each day.

Values: Criteria for Decision Making

A value is a decision-making principle: an articulation of what you want your decisions to accomplish. Identifying *loyalty* as a value demonstrates that your decisions will focus on honoring your connections and commitments. *Perseverance* says you'll choose to overcome obstacles and endure discomfort. *Mindfulness* says your decisions will aim to keep you conscious, aware, and engaged in any given moment.

When you identify your core values and take the time to define them, you are identifying the clear set of criteria you will use for decision making. Your values become the litmus test for the various options available to you: each potential course of action can be held up next to your list of identified values, allowing you to ask, "Which one of these options is most consistent with these values?"

Imagine for a moment you've identified the following

values (which are the three most common among respondents in my work) as fundamentally important to you and defined them as follows:

- **Honesty**—a commitment to fully providing information for which I am asked *or* that I know *should* be revealed.
- **Integrity**—a commitment to making decisions based on what I believe is the most respectable and respectful behavior rather than on potential benefits or consequences.
- **Family**—a commitment to making decisions that prioritize building and maintaining the strength, safety, and security of my family over any other considerations.

Now, imagine that you're working at a small business and your direct supervisor—someone you like tremendously and who is similarly popular with the rest of the staff—tasks you with installing some software on the company's network. As you begin to do so, it becomes clear that the software has been pirated and your company cannot legally install or use it. Assuming some sort of mistake has been made, you bring this to the attention of your supervisor, who gruffly denies there's any problem with the software and demands that you install it.

"Look," he says, "if you're not prepared or able to do the things I ask of you, I'm going to have to consider whether you're a great fit for this company."

You're in a tough situation, and after some thoughtful consideration of your options, you narrow your potential courses of action to the following:

1. Install the software as you've been asked.
2. Refuse to install the software and hope your supervisor asks someone else to do it.
3. Refuse to install the software and inform your direct supervisor's boss of the situation.
4. Install the software and a few weeks later call an anti-piracy tip line to let them know about the illegal software.

If you haven't clearly identified the core values that drive you as a leader, any number of criteria could be used to evaluate the best decision. If "will it result in me keeping my job" is the criteria against which options are measured, simply installing the software is likely your best option. However, then you've broken the law. If "will it keep me from doing something illegal" is your criteria, then refusing to install the software or informing your supervisor's boss is likely your best bet. However, those options could result in you or someone else getting fired, not to mention embroiling you in the middle of an uncomfortable situation with your supervisor and his boss. If your criteria is "will it help me stop something illegal with potentially no consequences to me," then anonymously calling the tip line might be your best bet. You've still done something illegal though, and there's always the possibility your supervisor will assume you were the one who tipped off the authorities. Let's not forget that since you were the one who installed the software, you may ultimately end up being held responsible!

Without a clearly defined set of core values, decision making requires two steps:

1. Identify the criteria you're going to use to evaluate your options.
2. Assess each option using that criteria.

Once you establish a core set of values, however, they *always* serve as your criteria for decision making. Decision making requires just one step: asking yourself "which of these options best lives up to my core values?"

Let's evaluate each of the four options in this scenario by asking "which one best lives up to the values of honesty, integrity, and family?"

Option 1—Install the software as you've been asked

Honesty—You know this is illegal and is denying people who created a product compensation for doing so. There could be serious consequences for the business if you are caught. According to your definition, honesty is about more than just providing truthful answers when asked: it demands you reveal things you know *should* be made known. This option simply doesn't live up to the value of honesty.

Integrity—While some illegal activities deserve respect (peaceful protests for instance), it's hard to make a case that using pirated software to save money is justifiable behavior. If you keep quiet it will be to avoid negative consequences to you personally, not because it is the right thing to do. That's not consistent with your definition of integrity.

Family—Choosing this option will make it less likely you will lose your job or deal with interpersonal issues that could hurt your career, which is better for your family's financial security. However, should your illegal activity be detected later, it could result in the weakening of family relationships due to a loss of respect and perhaps financial and legal penalties as well. Creating that sort of risk for your family means this option does not entirely live up to the value of family, though perhaps not as clearly as is the case with honesty and integrity.

Option 2—Refuse to install the software and hope your supervisor asks someone else

Honesty—You don't want to break the law and you are open about this with your supervisor. In this way this option respects your key value of honesty. However, the fact your supervisor is putting the company at risk with his illegal behavior is information his superiors should know for the good of the company and everyone who works there. Failing to reveal that information is being dishonest.

Integrity—Refusing to break the law personally is the proper thing to do, but someone of true integrity would take steps to ensure the crime doesn't happen at all. If integrity is important to you, you cannot choose this option.

Family—This option is the one most likely to cost you your job and impact your family's finances and security. Clearly it fails to honor this value.

Option 3—Refuse to install the software and inform your supervisor's boss of the situation

Honesty—You're straight with your supervisor and you make sure the company is protected. This option lives up to the value of honesty.

Integrity—This is a little more difficult, as what constitutes "respectable and respectful" behavior in this case is subjective. Some may argue that someone of integrity wouldn't "tattle" on their supervisor. Others may point out that your supervisor is being disrespectful to you, the law, and all the people at the company who could be negatively impacted if the unlawful behavior came to light. For the sake of this example, let's assume your perception of what's "right" is what will do the most potential good for the most people. If that's the case, this course of action lives up to the value of integrity.

Family—While this course of action will no doubt have an impact on some of your relationships at work, it seems unlikely to result in the loss of your job or anything else that could damage your family or its security.

Option 4—Install the software, and then a few weeks later call an anti-piracy tip line to let them know about the illegal software

Honesty—This option involves failing to reveal illegal activity, then hiding the fact from your supervisor that you are the person who called the tip line. It fails to live up to the value of honesty.

Integrity—The main goal of this option is avoiding personal consequences rather than behaving in a way that is right or respectable. As such, it fails to live up to the value of integrity.

Family—Should the call to the tip line result in an investigation, it's quite possible your involvement in installing the software could cost you your job and result in criminal and financial penalties. There is clearly a risk to your family relationships and security with this option.

When evaluated against the core values you've identified, it becomes clear only one option succeeds in honoring your values: refusing to install the software and informing your supervisor's boss about the situation.

The problem is that option sucks. Someone you previously liked and is popular with the rest of the staff is likely to be disciplined if not fired. Your supervisor is likely to be tremendously angry and blame you for any negative consequences he faces. The rest of the staff is going to know you went over your supervisor's head and some are likely to lose trust in or respect for you as a result. Your relationship with everyone at your current job is likely to change, in many cases not for the better.

This is the fundamental challenge with value-based decision making: it often results in short-term losses and unhappiness. Often the option most consistent with your values is not the one that brings the biggest rewards or avoids the most consequences. It may not allow you to get what you want, avoid embarrassment, or maintain a relationship.

However, the option most consistent with your values is

the one you are glad you chose five years in the future. Make every decision in life imagining how you would like to tell the story of that decision to a group of people you respect five years from now and a lot of the noise and confusion about what you should do in a given situation falls away.

Acting in a way that is inconsistent with your values takes an intellectual and emotional toll. It's not something you forget, and while losses suffered as a result of value-based decisions tend to alleviate over time (you get another job, you are forgiven by someone who was hurt by your decision, you start another relationship), the regret you feel over failing to live up to the person you hope to be rarely goes away. You may not think about it for a time, but every so often that decision will enter your consciousness and a feeling of disappointment in yourself will haunt you. Attach that feeling to enough of your decisions and it becomes increasingly difficult to see yourself as someone of whom you or anyone else should be proud.

Identifying the values you wish to use as your fundamental criteria for decision making is essential for anyone seeking to act as (and feel like) a leader on a daily basis. If you haven't clearly identified the values you want to drive you and taken the time to define them, what criteria *have* you been using to make decisions all these years?

For most of us, for most of our lives, the criteria we use to make decisions is simple:

Which option has the fewest negative consequences right now?

That criteria leads to inconsistent decision making that often lacks courage and integrity. Right now—on Day One— make a commitment to a new approach to decision making: evaluating options based on how well they live up to your clearly identified, clearly defined personal values. Good leaders do it because it allows them to live their values every time the opportunity presents itself. It's what I was doing when I used my original leadership philosophy (*What would the man I want to be do?*) to make decisions.

What separates great leaders from good leaders is this:

Good leaders live their values every time an opportunity presents itself. Great leaders create opportunities to live their values.

Great leaders create and act on a daily plan to ensure their behavior is consistent with the person they want to be. That's what sets the Day One leadership philosophy apart—it moves values-based leadership behaviors from reactive to proactive.

In the next chapter I'll teach you how to create and stick to that plan.

FIVE

Day One Leadership

A Personal Culture of Leadership

Day One Leadership starts with a plan. A plan to put the following process into action:

1. Identify a key value you wish to embody every day.
2. Clearly define that value.
3. Do something each day that embodies that value.

The third step is essential: only through disciplined repetition do your key leadership behaviors begin to happen unconsciously. When you no longer must consciously align your behavior with your values—when it happens by instinct—you have created a "personal culture of leadership."

Culture is a powerful force in determining behavior. What we wear, what we say, to what we aspire, and of what we are ashamed are all influenced by a fear of violating cultural expectations. Most of us have no control over the cultures into which we are born, but we can create the cultures in which we live and work by developing and consistently living up to clearly defined expectations for behavior each day.

The more decisions you make due to cultural expectations *you* had a hand in creating—rather than rules, policies, and procedures—the better off you are. Rules, policies, and procedures are easy to break. Everyone bends them, everyone breaks them, and forgiveness for those transgressions is built into our culture: if your violation isn't too serious, forgiveness can be assumed because "we've all been there." Violating a cultural expectation on the other hand brings with it swift and universal condemnation.

For instance, if you were attending an event at which I was the keynote speaker and heard me announce, "I received a speeding ticket on the way here this morning," you probably wouldn't think less of me as a person. However, if I took the stage without pants...well, then I've violated a cultural expectation and my guess is the decline in your opinion of me would be swift and precipitous. That's despite the fact the speed limit is a law designed to save lives and "you should wear pants" is an arbitrarily created expectation.

Day One leadership is about endeavoring to create a personal culture of leadership: a set of expectations for yourself that become so deeply engrained they begin to control your behavior in a positive way, every single day.

Living Up to Your Ideals

How do we go about beginning to create a personal culture of leadership? The Day One process began when a particularly dynamic student in our leadership program repeated a powerful quote: *"It's a lot easier to stand up for an ideal than it is to live up to one."*

At that moment a social experiment was born. I wanted to create a process that made people (myself included) actually live up to the things for which we claimed to stand. I chose a core group of students to pick one key value and make sure we "walked the walk" by living it each day.

Step one was picking the value. I challenged my students with the following scenario—I encourage you to consider your answer if it were to apply to your family, company, or community:

Imagine I give you the power to choose one value, and one value only. Whichever value you choose, every single person who is a member of this community will do at least one thing each day that embodies that value. It won't be the only value up to which people live, but it will be the only one that's guaranteed.

The students chose "impact."

Step two was clearly defining what "impact" meant. Our intention was to use the definition to guide our behavior, so I challenged my students to begin their definition with three words: "a commitment to." That phrase is almost always followed by a verb: a clearly defined action. They created the following: *"Impact is a commitment to creating moments that cause people to feel better off for having interacted with you."*

The experiment was supposed to be simple enough: each student was responsible for doing at least one thing each day that created a moment of impact as we had defined it. They were to stop by my office before they left campus to let me know what they had done. I committed to doing the same thing.

It didn't take long for me to notice something, however: before they'd enter my office to provide their update the students would pause in my outer office for a few moments. I could see them thinking back over their day to identify a moment that satisfied the criteria we had established for impact. Inevitably they found one and reported it to me, but it was clear that they hadn't thought about the assignment all day. Instead, they were looking back and trying spot impact in behavior that had *already happened*. I have to admit I was doing the same thing. We had hoped this key value of "impact" would *drive* new behaviors and influence our decisions as we made them. Instead, the only new behavior was an extra stop by my office each day.

We needed a different approach and it was born from a combination of two psychological phenomena: the Zeigarnik effect and the question-behavior effect (QBE).

The Zeigarnik effect (named for Bluma Zeigarnik, a student of legendary psychologist Kurt Lewin) notes that you're more likely to remember an incomplete or interrupted task than you are a task you've already completed. In other words, things you haven't done assume a more prominent position in your consciousness than those you have.[2]

The question-behavior effect (first demonstrated by Jim Sherman at Indiana University) holds that asking people questions about a behavior ahead of time can actually lead to a change in behavior later on.

Sherman asked one group of subjects to predict how likely there were to engage in two types of behaviors: those that society would deem "desirable" and those that society would deem "undesirable." He asked no such questions of another group. Upon evaluating the behaviors of the two groups later on, those who were asked questions about their anticipated future behavior were far more likely to have engaged in socially desirable behavior and far less likely to have engaged in undesirable behavior.[3]

These two psychological effects got me thinking: if an unfinished task was going to be top of mind (anyone who has ever tried to truly enjoy some Netflix with an essay still to write, a project to complete, or an inbox to empty knows exactly what I'm talking about) and questions about desired future behavior could actually cause it to happen, why don't we see if posing a specific question about impact is a more powerful driver of value-consistent behavior than the approach we were taking?

This approach changed everything. We created a question that was carefully crafted so that to answer it you would need to actually *do* something. The key was this: in the process of doing that "something" you would embody our definition of "impact."

We brainstormed. We created, refined, and dismissed ideas. Finally, we had the question we were looking for:

"What have I done today to recognize someone else's leadership?"

Our thinking was simple: it was unlikely someone would walk away from an interaction in which they were called a leader without feeling better off for having had that interaction. You couldn't answer the question without creating an impact.

The beautiful thing was the question was extremely broad—there were countless different ways it could be answered. Everyone seeking an answer could define leadership however they chose to do so. It allowed them to recognize others' leadership verbally, in written form, openly, or anonymously. We had been whiteboarding all along, and when we stepped back, the following was on the board:

> **VALUE**: *Impact*
> **DEFINITION**: A commitment to *creating moments that cause people to feel better off for having interacted with you.*
> **QUESTION**: *What have I done today to recognize someone else's leadership?*

Each of us committed to answering the question each day for a week. We made it an obligation to ourselves: it wasn't something we would take care of "if time permitted"—it was to be prioritized at the very top of our to-do lists each day.

I had no idea just how transformative that simple question would prove to be.

Finding Leadership

The next evening, I found myself in a packed grocery store. The kind of packed that makes you want to simply turn around and walk out, but damn it I needed that peanut butter.

I found myself in the shortest line, which was still almost twenty people long. Glancing up for a moment I caught a glimpse of the young woman operating the cash register. She was quite simply the greatest cashier I had ever seen. Her arms were a blur as she fired items across the scanner at breakneck speed. Everything beeped, everything found its way into a bag in an instant. This woman was a checkout ninja.

It occurred to me how unusual it was to think to myself,

"That woman is the greatest cashier I've ever seen." Unfortunately, the more people in our society we believe capable of doing a job, the less likely we are to recognize excellence in that job. There are magazines and websites dedicated to debating the Top 50 athletes/musicians/business titans of all time, but with cashiers, serving staff, bus drivers, janitors, and even (inexplicably in my mind) teachers and nurses, there's too often a perception that "anyone can do those jobs." As such, it seems we treat high performance in those jobs as somehow a lower class of excellence.

Standing in line watching that extraordinary cashier, I realized: *"This is the perfect opportunity to answer that question we created."*

I determined that when I finally reached the end of the line I would tell her that seeing someone so committed to her work was a perfect example of what I thought leadership was all about. I would tell her that anyone so skillful and dedicated to their work helping others was a leader, and that I noticed and appreciated it.

Then for twenty minutes I watched people treat her like dirt. There are few things that bring out the worst in human beings more than standing in line, and perhaps it was the fact this transaction was the last thing standing between a lot of these people and a long weekend, but not only did no one acknowledge how hard this woman was working, many didn't even recognize she was in front of them *at all*. The impatient sighs and audible grumbles were bad enough, but many stared through her, talked on the phone, or kept their eyes on their grocery bags even as they handed over cash and credit cards.

Yet the cashier never slowed down. She never stopped

greeting each person as they moved through the line, even when the response was nothing more than a grunt (if they bothered to provide one at all). She continued to send people out the door ten minutes faster than if they had been in any other line.

When I reached the front of the line I tried to make eye contact as she greeted me. When I did, I saw profound exhaustion and frustration. In that moment I determined I wasn't just going to *say* something nice to her, I wanted to *do* something nice for her.

I turned to the candy shelves next to the checkout and asked, "Excuse me, but which of these chocolates do you think are the best?" I was shocked by the aggressiveness with which she snapped back, "The caramels!"

There are certain words in the English language you never expect to hear snapped at you in anger. "Caramels" is on that list.

Undeterred, I put the caramels on the checkout belt and watched as she rang them up and went to put them into my bag.

"Actually," I said, stopping her. "I got those for you. I have to tell you you're the very best at this job I've ever seen. My job is to teach leadership and the way you're approaching your job is exactly the type of example I use for what real leadership looks like."

I gestured at the long line that still lay behind me.

"I've been watching, and I've seen that no one has really given you the credit you deserve for it, so I thought you deserved some chocolates."

I smiled, hoping that she'd smile back. She started to cry. Not what I was going for.

As a Canadian, I've apologized to inanimate objects over

which I have tripped. To see a woman crying in front of me because of something I've said…well, it triggered an avalanche of apologies. She held up her hand to cut me off.

"No sir, please don't apologize," she said, wiping her eyes. "It's just that no one has even been polite to me today…and you bought me chocolates? I just don't know how to deal with this."

I started that interaction to live up to my commitment to act on a key personal value. As I walked away I realized what a profound impact it had on both me and that cashier. Up until that point, had her family asked how her day was when she got home, it's quite possible she would have snapped at them and passed along that lack of consideration and respect she'd experienced time and time again from those of us in line. Now I realized that even if not a single additional positive thing happened to her all day, she was going to lead with "This guy did the nicest thing for me today!"

For me, her response brought a realization: I had been letting a lot of similar opportunities for impact pass me by. I had identified a small percentage of my daily interactions as important and, outside of those interactions, tended to let my focus rest on my phone, my to-do list and the things I felt I had to do to excel at my job. That moment was a reminder that every interaction was a chance to model the leadership I hoped to see from my students.

If you want to model your leadership more consistently be more conscious about looking for and recognizing the leadership of others. Look for leaders like that cashier: those whose behavior goes beyond what is expected and reminds you of what's possible.

Leadership recognized is leadership created. That cashier's

actions led me to recognize her leadership and my recognition made it more likely she'd repeat those actions. Leadership is created and reinforced through this cycle. You're surrounded by people who go beyond what is expected in your workplace and community, so you're surrounded by leaders. Start looking for and recognizing them, and we can keep that cycle moving.

SIX

Operationalizing Your Leadership Values

My students had leaned into this assignment: creating remarkable stories of seeking out and recognizing leaders in their lives, past and present. Coaches, teachers, parents, even the wildly friendly hot dog vendor on campus had been told "you are a leader" in profoundly meaningful ways. That single question had changed a lot of lives in only seven days.

One of my shyest and most brilliant students (we'll call him Aaron) shared a story that truly moved me. Aaron had waited at his old bus stop for the man who had driven him to elementary school when he was a kid. When the bus pulled up, Aaron waited for the children to board and then stepped on the bus himself.

"What are you doing?" the elementary school bus driver naturally asked a twenty-two-year-old.

"Sir, you drove me to school for nine years," Aaron told him. "Back then I was incredibly fat and really, really smart."

Any of you who have lived through that combination know how difficult that experience can be for a kid.

"I was bullied so badly I had to stand in the front hallway of my house and cry as hard as I could for thirty seconds before I could walk outside every morning," continued Aaron. "Then I'd wait at this stop, you'd pull up, and I'd sit up in the front because all the cool kids sat in the back.

"And you'd sing Disney songs all the way to school, every day. And you were terrible, and the kids in the back mocked you constantly. You heard them, and you never seemed to care. What those kids thought was so important to me and watching you not care about what they said about you—watching you just keep smiling and singing—on so many days, it's what convinced me I could get through just one more day of their crap.

"Sir," Aaron told him, "I go to Harvard for grad school next year. You're as big a part of that as any person in my life. I never said thank you. I never told you you're one of the greatest leaders I know."

When pressed about how the bus driver responded, Aaron simply smiled and said, "He appreciated it."

More than a dozen of us participated in this experiment and each one had created a moment like that every day for a week. Those 100+ moments of impact were worth celebrating, but the more important lesson is this: we recognized each one of those leaders in our lives once, but we did so because they had impacted us many, many times, and most of those times went unrecognized. Until we looked for those moments of leadership, we didn't see them. Until we recognized they were moments of leadership, neither did the people who created them.

Most of the leadership on the planet comes from people who don't see themselves as leaders. Aaron's bus driver and the cashier I spoke with are examples of the world's most abundant type of leader: people who impact others by doing more than what is expected. Those in this group often feel the jobs they do and the positions they hold don't qualify for the title of leader. You may be one of them.

Leaders aren't identified by their jobs, they're identified by how they choose to do them. When you do your job and live your life in a way that impacts others positively, you're a leader—whether your job is commanding an aircraft carrier or getting someone's child home safely after school. Many people don't believe that, so we need to tell them. In doing so we live our own leadership. The cycle continues—but we must be consistent at reinforcing it.

The Day One approach is how you make your most beneficial leadership behaviors more consistent. Embedding that question into our lives didn't change who were or what we valued: we had always been kind people who wanted to have a positive impact. It did make us *behave* more consistently in ways that reflected who we were and what we valued. It forced us to look for the leaders surrounding us each day; it showed us how many opportunities for impact we were ignoring; and it made it far less likely we would continue to allow those opportunities to pass us by.

We adopted the mindset that every day we had to *earn* another day on this planet: we didn't get to wake up the next morning unless we could pass a test at the end of the day. However, it was only a one-question test, and we were given the question at the beginning of the day: *What have I done today to recognize someone else's leadership?* We had all day to provide an answer to that question, knowing that if we failed we didn't earn another spin around the sun. Each day was Day One and the next Day One had to be earned.

I was impacted so significantly by the effectiveness of this approach that I've been living and teaching the process ever since. I named it "Operationalizing Leadership Values" and it's where you start on Day One—creating the foundation of a leadership of which we are all capable, to which we should all commit, and that we can all celebrate.

In Part III, I'm going to show you exactly how to customize this process for your own life. I'm going to walk you step-by-step through the process of identifying your personal leadership values and teach you how to choose or create the questions that embed those values into your life and work. I'll show you how to adapt your behavior to be more congruent with the person you want to be.

But first, in Part II, I want to share with you my journey through the process and the extraordinary leadership lessons it taught me.

PART II

Six Key Leadership Values

SEVEN

The Big Six

Every single day I tell myself "this is Day One"—I imagine that every accomplishment I've ever had, every mistake I've ever made, every good and bad thing I've ever done has been wiped clean and I get to start fresh today building myself into the type of person I want to be. This means I can't rest on my laurels from the past and can't worry about things beyond my control in the future. All I need to focus on is what I accomplish today and ensuring that it's in line with the person I want to be.

In Part I, I introduced the process I use to do that—operationalizing leadership values. It's a process with three steps:

1. Identify a key value.
2. Clearly define what that value means.
3. Operationalize that value by turning it into an action-oriented question you answer each day.

I was impressed by the effectiveness of our first attempt to operationalize the value of "impact," but it was my students who had chosen that value. I wanted to start living a life focused around my own personal values in addition to our collective value of impact.

This is the story of how the six key leadership values (and accompanying questions) that drive my life on a daily basis emerged. My questions have evolved and changed over time, but the process you'll learn in Part III brought clarity and consistency, and today each of my Day Ones have six consistent values and questions:

1. Impact—What have I done today to recognize someone else's leadership?
2. Courage—What did I try today that might not work, but I tried it anyway?
3. Empowerment—What did I do today to move someone else closer to a goal?
4. Growth—What did I do today to make it more likely someone will learn something?
5. Class—When did I elevate instead of escalate today?
6. Self-Respect—What did I do today to be good to myself?

These aren't the only six values I care about and the answers to the six questions through which they're operationalized aren't the only priorities I have each day, but these six values and the questions which accompany them have become the foundation of every single day of my life. They ensure consistency and momentum, and since committing to them I've seen tremendous gains personally and professionally.

I live every day like it's Day One—and these six values drive my behavior for every one of those Day Ones. They were the catalysts for this book and they're the reason I've had the opportunity to speak to hundreds of thousands of people around the world. They're the reason I was able to lose a hundred pounds, stay committed to my sobriety, and achieve financial security doing what I love (though I hope by the end of this book you don't equate cash with credibility).

All of that has happened since I first implemented this process almost a decade ago. I want to share these six transformative leadership values, the questions that embed them in my life, and the countless leadership lessons I have learned through their creation and daily implementation. Then I will help you discover your key values and create your personal daily leadership questions. I will show you the process I used to change my life and grow my leadership. When coupled with the lessons of this section, you'll not only feel like a leader by the end of this book, you'll be acting like one.

EIGHT

Impact

A commitment to creating moments that cause people to feel they are better off having interacted with you.

QUESTION: What have I done today to recognize someone else's leadership?

If you're going to start with a single question on Day One, start with this one. If you make this question a part of your life for thirty days, it will be a month of tremendous leadership generation on your part.

This question puts you on the lookout for moments of leadership. It makes it more likely you will examine the people with whom you interact each day and ask, "Who is creating moments that send others away feeling better than before?" More importantly, it ensures that when you do identify those individuals, you will be likely to seize the opportunity to recognize them, learn from them, and reinforce the behaviors that impressed you.

Just

If you're looking for a simple key to act as a trigger for opportunities to answer this question, might I suggest being on the lookout for a single word—"just."

The English language is a language of qualifiers: "perhaps," "maybe," "possibly," "potentially." Each of those words is used as a replacement for "yes" because they provide more wiggle room: we always want to qualify our commitment to a task. We do the same thing when we evaluate ourselves and what we do: add qualifiers and limiting words. "Just" is one of the most prevalent and restrictive of them.

Our lives and organizations are filled with "I'm just a..." people. "I'm just a receptionist"; "I'm just a salesperson"; "I'm just middle management"; "I'm just a stay-at-home mom"; "I'm just part-time"; "I'm just a student." It's likely that each one of us has said something similar about ourselves or, at the very least, about something we were attempting to do: "I'm just trying to get to the end of this project"; "We just have to figure out a way to deal with this."

Every time we use the word "just" to describe who we are or what we're doing, we're telling people that we are unimportant. Every time we say we're "just" something, we're giving people permission to expect less from us.

Our lives and workplaces are filled with extraordinary people who regularly diminish themselves in this way and in the process, many convince themselves that it's true. As such, I believe that one of the simplest but most powerful things we can do to enhance our leadership is to refuse to allow people who we know are people of value to diminish themselves in front of us.

A commitment to banishing the word "just" from our vocabulary and our workplaces can have a profound impact. After all, in many organizations the employees who have the most consistent contact with those outside the organization (and therefore play the biggest role in what people think about an organization) are often those who are paid the least. Even those who take pride in their job and recognize they make valuable contributions do not miss the fact that their position has been judged less monetarily valuable. No matter how hard we try or how little sense it makes, we cannot seem to avoid allowing our sense of self-worth to be tied to where we fall on the spectrum of financial compensation.

Each of us can play a small role in helping to counteract this phenomenon and help ensure that the leadership of those who say they're "just" something is recognized by others, and by themselves. You'd be shocked just how incongruent a leader's true impact and their conception of that impact can actually be—a fact of which I was reminded on a trip back to my old high school.

Mr. Peters

I don't care who you are or how accomplished you've become, when you walk through the doors of your old school you revert to the person you were all those years ago. High school wasn't the easiest time in the world for me. While I collected an impressive collection of awards and accolades, I was profoundly insecure. I had been overweight most of my life, and while I thinned out in high school I never stopped seeing myself as the fat kid who was mocked throughout elementary school. Terrified of a fashion faux pas with my hair or clothing,

I simply shaved my head and wore my football jersey most days. I had friends but didn't feel like I was a part of any of the school's groups. I didn't attend my first party until senior year.

There was someone who made my experience better: a man by the name of Mr. Peters (not his real name, he'd impale me on a mop if I used his real name). Mr. Peters was one of the custodians at our school. He had been there for over twenty years and was one of the most remarkably kind men with whom I have ever crossed paths. He knew every student's name, congratulated people on their athletic achievements and acceptance to universities, and took tremendous pleasure in the growth and happiness of the people after whom he mopped up. Most impressively, though, he had an incredible ability to know which of us felt bullied, alienated, insecure, or left out, and he made a point of stopping on his rounds to talk to us. He would always remember the last conversation we'd had, and he'd reference it to pick up the next one. Remembering people's names is one thing, but that reference to where we left off last time—to this day it's something I try to do. It's a remarkably powerful tool for connection. A lot of days in high school were made better because of this man. There were many moments through which I didn't think I could make it when a kind word or gesture from Mr. Peters made a huge difference.

As I waited in the principal's office before heading down to the presentation (an odd sensation at the age of thirty-five), I was shocked when Mr. Peters spotted me through the window, beelined into the office, and embraced me in a huge hug.

"Drew Dudley!" he bellowed. "It's so great to see you!"

My jaw dropped. It had been a decade and a half since I

had seen this man. He worked in a place that had more than 1,200 students walking the halls each year and he remembered me?

"Mr. Peters!" I sputtered. "I can't believe you remember my name!"

He looked shocked. "Remember your name?" he replied. "Drew, I've been following your whole career! I'm so proud of you!"

Two things happen when someone unexpectedly tells you "I'm proud of you" and you know they mean it:

1. You instinctively go "Awwww." Sometimes it's out loud, sometimes it's in a deep recess of your brain, but you do it.
2. You immediately begin to think about the many individuals in your life of whom you are tremendously proud.

All of us have people in our lives of whom we are proud. However, when was the last time the phrase, "I am so proud of you" actually escaped your lips? "I am so proud of you," when spoken honestly, is almost impossible to hear without feeling as if your day is fundamentally better. It creates a moment of impact. It creates a moment of leadership. My guess is that you have been sitting on one of those potential moments of leadership each day, but you haven't taken time to consciously act on it. You've been meaning to do it; you've been hoping to do it; but you haven't been planning to do it.

That's the power of questions like "What have I done today to recognize someone else's leadership?" It acts as a prompt for behavior of which we're capable but often fail to make time for. You could get up tomorrow morning and decide, "I'm going to call the first boss I had and tell them how much their mentorship and advice have meant to my career." Sometimes that's how the questions work—they act as a catalyst for creating a situation in which we answer them. Other times a situation in which we find ourselves reminds us of the question, which spurs us to answer it. That was the case as I stood looking at Mr. Peters. As his kind words sunk in I realized I couldn't miss this opportunity to recognize him as a leader.

"Mr. Peters," I said. "I'm about to give a speech on leadership. In fact, some of the biggest companies in the world pay me to talk about leadership. I want you to know that the type of leadership I focus on is the type that you embody every day. It's about being committed to finding a way to make a positive impact each day, one person at a time. You always did that, but I didn't realize at the time that it truly was leadership. I do now, and I wanted to tell you that you are one of the most amazing leaders I know. Thanks for that."

I don't know what I expected his response to be. Perhaps another hug? Instead, he smiled wryly and gave a dismissive shrug.

"Aw," he said, "I'm just a janitor lucky enough to know all of you before you hit the big time."

"Just a janitor."

Our lives and workplaces are filled with too many people who think like that. Who have convinced themselves that they have no right to think of themselves as leaders because of what job they've ended up doing, or where in the corporate hierarchy they appear to have peaked. What's more, according to the social rules we've accepted, Mr. Peters' perspective makes total sense: I'd worked hard to get great grades and earn scholarships to good schools. I'd done the things necessary to win awards, get promotions, and eventually start my own company. With every step in my career, there were fewer and fewer people like me. The rules say that makes me more valuable, and that's what he was acknowledging. Those rules convince us it makes more sense to chase money and titles than it does to chase what Mr. Peters has achieved, but what he has achieved needs to be better acknowledged. Thousands of students have walked the halls of my old high school. Thousands of them have become the friend of Mr. Peters. They have gone on to be doctors and lawyers and CEOs—the people the rules say deserve our admiration and respect. Over the course of my work, I've reached out to many of the most successful individuals with whom I went to high school. I've visited their corner offices and interviewed them about their perceptions of leadership, the values that drive them and the questions they ask themselves each day to ensure they live those values. At some point in every one of those interviews I make sure I ask the question, "Hey, do you remember Mr. Peters?"

Each and every one of them smiles when they hear his name. Twenty years or more after they last saw the man, they smile at the mere mention of his name. That to me is a remarkable life. That is a life of leadership.

Our value is not measured by how well we become one of the few. Our lives and our organizations are filled with leaders who have adopted that perspective and as such refuse to acknowledge their role as leaders. What if we all worked to create a culture in which the true measure of our lives is how many people smile when our name is spoken twenty years after they last saw us? What if we could aim to live a life and create workplaces where that objective is advanced as our primary motivation?

How do we identify and recognize the unsung leaders in our lives and organizations? I do it by asking this question: If I was not permitted to consider wealth, position, or prestige—if those things were no longer part of the equation—who would I look up to? Who lives their life in a way I tremendously admire? For me, it would be Mr. Peters.

It's important we identify the people in our lives and organizations who are living their lives in ways that impress us and take a moment to let them know we see them as leaders. Not just tell them that we value them, or that what they do matters, or that we care about them but that they are *leaders* to us.

"How have I recognized someone else's leadership today?"

Again, make asking this question an obligation to yourself for thirty days. Answering it will create moments of impact that remind others they have mattered, do matter, and will matter in the future. To do that for others is certainly leadership in and of itself, but what's more important is that those moments will be passed on by those who receive them. A single daily question will begin to generate ripples of impact throughout lives and communities—ripples that will start with you. That's leadership—and there's no reason not to start now.

Five Ways You Can Embody *Impact* Today (on Day One)

1. Be on the lookout for the word "just." Politely remind anyone who uses it that they're not "just" anything.
2. Identify someone in the service industry with whom you interact regularly and let them know the way they do their job makes your day a little better.
3. Locate a former teacher who made a difference in your life and let them know you still think about their lessons.
4. Learn the name and birthday of a homeless person you see each day.
5. Post a profile of a leader in your life and how they've impacted you on social media. Don't tell them but tag them.

Questions You Could Ask to Operationalize *Impact*:

- What did I do to recognize someone else's leadership today?
- What conscious act of kindness did I perform today?
- What did I do today to show someone that they matter?
- How did I create a "lollipop moment" for someone today?

NINE

Courage

A commitment to taking action when there is a possibility of loss.

QUESTION: What did I try today that I thought might not work, but I tried it anyway?

Rejection Therapy

As of the writing of this book, my friend Ammad has interviewed over 250 of the most successful leaders on the planet. He asks them all the same set of questions, and once he hits 1,000 interviews, he plans on sharing what he's found with the world. After our interview, I asked him if he'd share with me just one of the more interesting insights he'd heard.

"Rejection therapy," he replied.

Entrepreneur Jason Comely had shared with Ammad his concept of "rejection therapy"—actively seeking out rejection to not only develop a resilience to it, but to turn it into a positive experience.[4] I remember thinking it was a fascinating idea and immediately hatched a plan to start doing it myself. Then I promptly forgot about it.

A few months later, while chatting with one of the young cofounders of a successful media company, I asked him what his most important tip would be for leaders trying to develop courage and resilience.

He leaned forward and said, without hesitation, "rejection therapy." There it was again! I asked him to expand a little on how he understood it.

"Look," he replied. "My partner and I have never been cool. At all. How other people viewed us seemed like a big deal for a long time. We cared whether or not we were accepted. Generally, we knew that we weren't, and we were constantly afraid of rejection. Rejection from the cool kids, rejection from girls, rejection of the things we thought we could build.

"The problem," he continued, "is it didn't take long once we started a business for us to realize that if we were afraid of rejection, everything was going to have to be perfect before we launched it and as soon as anything we did was accepted, we'd be afraid to change it. You can't innovate without change, and you won't change if you're afraid of rejection. So, we knew we simply had to get better at it.

"But you can't just decide to be better at something," he pointed out. "If you want to get better at anything in the world, you've got to practice it. We decided to start practicing rejection."

"What does it look like exactly?" I asked.

He laughed. "Honestly," he said, "we turned it into a

competition. We dedicate one day each month to competing to see which one of us can get rejected more times in a twenty-four-hour period. Whoever loses has to buy dinner for an entire month."

"What happens on those days?" I asked.

"I have a date every weekend," he said smiling, "because on that one day I walk up to the most beautiful people I can find and just ask them to go out to dinner with me. For most of them, the first response is 'I don't even know you.' I just tell them that once every month I spend a day trying to get rejected because it makes me a better person. Most of them find that really interesting. Honestly, I wish I could go back and tell my high school self that as you get older, interesting is a hell of a lot more important than hot!

"It's been amazing what we've gotten to do," he continued. "We'll walk into a sub shop and ask, 'Can we make our own sandwich?' The guy behind the counter doesn't care! We've walked up to police officers and asked if we could shoot at stop signs like they did in *Superbad*!"

He told me that through their experiences they had learned three important truths:

1. You don't get rejected nearly as often as you think you will. Sometimes you actually have to work at it.

2. If you expect to get rejected it has no impact on your self-worth when it happens. In fact, it's kind of funny. Eventually you start feeling that way about rejection every day.

3. Even when you are rejected you are usually offered something better than what you currently have.

"There was no way the cops were going to let us shoot anything," he told me. "But they did let us drive their cruiser, so that was pretty cool!"

Confidence vs. Courage

I had a buddy in university who never seemed to have a problem with dating. He was always surrounded by the most extraordinary women—smart, funny, beautiful. I asked him once how he managed, and he shrugged and gave me the same answer those of us intimidated by dating have heard again and again.

"Confidence my friend. Confidence is sexy."

It never rang true to me. Now I think I know why. Confidence can be faked, and all too often slips into cockiness or arrogance. Engaging in rejection therapy doesn't require confidence, what it requires is *courage*. Confidence is acting like something doesn't scare you. Courage is *doing* something that *does* scare you. You can have confidence without action, but courage is only demonstrated *through* action.

Leaders are always scared. They simply don't let fear lead to inaction. The challenges that scare us can be as benign as asking someone out or as profound as facing a cancer diagnosis. Regardless of where on that spectrum our fears fall, it's courage that allows us to act in the face of those fears.

Courage takes practice and embedding it into your life daily provides you with evidence you can face ever-larger challenges. Don't wait until you need courage to discover how much you have: develop it every day so you understand the depth of your capacity. For that you need a tool: the right daily question.

I discovered my courage-driving question when I faced one of my biggest fears: attending my first support group meeting for my alcohol addiction. I didn't walk straight into that meeting. I knew I had to go and I was convinced I was going to go until I got to the door. Then I stopped dead. I had all these hopes for success and accomplishment in my life and it seemed to me that walking through that door, acknowledging I was an alcoholic, and officially accepting "help" would mean that I was opening myself up to negative judgment—my own and others—for the rest of my life.

I stood there frozen. The woman holding the door smiled at me. No doubt she'd seen this kind of hesitation from people before.

After a moment she put her hand on my shoulder and said, "Still thinking about it?"

I looked at her. "Yeah, look, honestly, I just don't think this is going to work for me."

She looked back for a moment before saying, "Well, why not try this: just say to yourself 'I don't think this is going to work, but I'm going to try it anyway.'"

So, I did. I said to myself, "I don't think this is going to work. But I'm going to try it anyway," and walked in the door.

That phrase probably saved my life. From that day on it's been my action-oriented question for catalyzing courage in my life every day. It's a question you must ask again and again if you truly want to get the most from it. Walking in that door the first time wasn't enough: I had to keep asking that question over and over as I've worked to remain sober, build my company, and find ways to continue to grow as a person.

Later in my journey I told a woman about how hesitant I was at that first doorway—how I almost refused the help that might save my career and my life because I thought it might make me look bad. She smiled and told me something I've never forgotten: "The need to save face keeps a lot of people from asking for the help they need. When you're in deep you can save face, or you can save your ass, but you don't get to do both. Choose wisely."

It's courage that defines leaders, not confidence. Courage is a commitment to taking action when there is a possibility of loss. Sometimes the potential loss is of something tangible: money, a job, or an opportunity. More often than not the potential loss that keeps us from acting is really a perceived loss: a loss of face. Losing face means losing respect or prestige in the eyes of *others*. If we continually hesitate to act because of concerns about what others think of us, our perception of and respect for ourselves will continually erode.

Only through demonstrating courage each day—not to others, but to yourself—will you start to recognize that the positive self-worth generated from daily acts of courage far outstrips any reputational losses that occur from your failures. Any reputational losses you do suffer will tend to be in the eyes of individuals with whom you rarely interact—often only once. If someone only sees one instance of you "trying something that might not work" and indeed it doesn't work, they may very well think less of you in that moment. Most people with whom you only interact once don't play a significant role in your life, however, and it's wise to remember Eleanor Roosevelt's observation that "you wouldn't worry so much about what other people think of you if you realized how seldom they do."

People who do interact with you regularly will see constant demonstrations of courage—a constant willingness to try something despite the possibility of loss. They'll see you are committed to growth, to challenge, and to focusing more on what you can learn and achieve than what others think of you. What will stick with them is not the outcomes of your attempts (though, as noted above, they generally yield far more than expected) but the commitment you have to your own values. Is the judgment of people you will see only once worth giving up that kind of respect from those around you and, more importantly, from yourself?

"What have I tried today that I thought might not work but I tried it anyway?"

I've gotten backstage tours, made flight announcements, eaten at chefs' tables, met stars, driven race cars, and even flown in private planes because of that question. It has been a constant source of personal growth and prepared me to make decisions in the face of much more significant consequences than walking through a door. I know that I'm capable of courage when I need it because I've been practicing for a long time.

Let me be clear: it was *not* easy to make answering that question a daily commitment. I had no idea how powerful my instincts to avoid loss had become. I wanted to take risks but was quite simply afraid—even if the losses would be small or entirely private. No doubt there are doubts in your mind as well. Why are they so powerful, and what can we use to overcome them?

The Magic Question

A few years back a young man approached me after a guest lecture at a university.

"Mr. Dudley," he began, "my friend would really like to talk to you, but he has really powerful social anxiety. We're all kind of surprised he came tonight. Would you be willing to spend a couple of minutes with him? He's an amazing guy, but it might be a little awkward."

I've dealt with anxiety at times in my life and have some tremendous friends who continue to battle it, so I indicated I was more than happy to talk. The young man beckoned to his friend, who shuffled over staring at the floor. We began to chat, and he could not have been nicer, although every couple of minutes he had to walk away, gather himself, and come back to resume the conversation. Each time he would apologize profusely for the interruption.

Finally, I said, "Look, my friend, you really don't have to apologize. I know how difficult dealing with this can be. I know that it takes an awful lot of courage to come up and talk with a complete stranger."

He nodded, still looking at the floor.

"Mr. Dudley," he finally said, "dealing with this for so long has taught me something pretty simple: the quality of my life is really going to depend on how often I'm willing to ask myself, 'Am I capable of five seconds of extraordinary courage right now?'"

Am I capable of five seconds of extraordinary courage right now?

I've probably repeated that question to myself thousands of times in the years since. I've asked it as I've waited backstage moments before a presentation, when I asked the love of my life to dinner for the first time, and basically every time I sat down to write a single line of this book. The wonderful thing about that question is the answer is always yes. We are all capable of five seconds of courage at any given moment—the question is simply a reminder of that fact.

Don't get me wrong, we may not have the courage to deal with what might happen five minutes after we show that courage, or with what might happen the next day, month, or year, but that's not what the question is asking you to assess. It's asking you if you've got five seconds worth of extraordinary courage *right now*—in this moment. We've all got five seconds within us at any given time. Accept that fact and the number of things of which you're capable grows exponentially.

The challenge is we're not trained to look at the five seconds in front of us. Which is too bad because they're not all that scary. What are scary are the *perceived* consequences we create in our minds about what might happen *after* the five seconds.

"He's going to laugh at me for showing I'm interested."

"I'm going to get fired for speaking up."

"If this is the wrong decision, I'm going to be setting myself back years."

None of those things can happen in the five seconds in front of us, they're all down the road. Some might be just a few moments down the road, others might be years away, but the fact remains—it's not that you doubt your ability to accept the challenge directly in front of you, it's that you doubt your ability to withstand the potential consequences of doing so.

It's natural to look down the road. Just remember that road is yours: it's supposed to be created *by you* as you move along. Your life isn't supposed to unfold according to a specific template, and leaders consciously ensure it doesn't do so. That's a challenge because for many of us fortunate enough to live in the developed world, our future is mapped out more than it's actively created. Certain goals and milestones for our future are clearly identified for us as we grow up: degrees, jobs, marriage, and children, in a certain order and by a certain time. This keeps us looking ahead and evaluating every decision based on whether it will help us hit benchmarks on a timeline created for us by others. This generates fear in every decision—not because we don't think we're capable of making the decision, but because we're afraid of what might happen *after* we do. We learn to try to avoid mistakes instead of recognizing that we possess the courage to make them and the resilience to recover from them. A key generator of this fear is implanted early on. I call it "the list" and it's often a destroyer of leadership.

The List

I met Alison Ellwood when a mutual friend asked me to help raise funds for Alison's cross-Canada bike ride. Alison's aim was to collect the stories of women who had battled and beaten breast cancer. Inspired by her own mother's battle with the disease and the strength she had drawn from hearing the stories of other survivors, Alison's hope was to compile the stories she collected into a book that could be distributed to women when they received their diagnosis.

"When a woman is told she has breast cancer, it's going to be one of the scariest days of her life," she told me. "I want those women to be able to feel the same hope and strength that was shared with my mother."

The voyage took three months and covered almost 5,000 miles, a good portion of it alone. It was a remarkable display of passion and commitment, one I felt was worth sharing with the students in the leadership program at the University of Toronto. I invited Alison to come and share her story.

That night, in front of 200 mostly first- and second-year students, Alison told the story of her struggle to make the trip a reality: the fights for funding, the grueling physical training, and the challenge of getting her parents on board with the thought of their twenty-three-year-old daughter spending twelve weeks pedaling Canada's highways (not all of which are anywhere near something resembling civilization).

As she shared the physical, mental, and emotional hardships and triumphs that emerged over three months crossing the world's second-largest country, I watched the students start to look at her as someone to admire and emulate. Until she took the first question at the end of the presentation. A first-year student raised his hand and asked, "Where did you go to school?" As if it somehow bore some impact on the validity of everything she had just shared.

Alison laughed. "A better question would be, where *didn't* I go to school!" she replied. "I dropped out of several schools before I ended up at the place I graduated."

The audience's reaction is one I will never forget. Some had a look of horror on their faces. Others shook their head as if disappointed in her. I caught at least a couple rolling their eyes and closing their notebooks. The overall message was clear: this woman has no credibility in our eyes. I couldn't understand it. A story of extraordinary tenacity, strength, and courage—and the fact that she dropped out of university undermined everything she had to say? In a single instant she had gone from someone to admire to a cautionary tale. It was at that moment when I realized how powerful "the list" is.

We carry a subconscious list of the things we believe we must accomplish to feel like and be considered a success. This list is learned without being overtly taught and is so powerfully ingrained in our psyche that any deviation from this list—no matter how exciting or potentially gratifying—is seen as foolish or even reckless. It is built on the premise that while there may be many paths to success, there is one well-established, continually validated path that pretty much *guarantees* success if we're just willing to be disciplined and put in the work necessary to follow it.

Following that path simply demands that you follow the list:

1. Go to kindergarten and play nice.
2. Go to elementary school and do what the teachers tell you.
3. Go to high school so that you can go to a good university (which usually means doing what the teachers tell you).
4. Go to university so that you can get a really good entry-level job (which usually means figuring out what the professor wants you to tell them).
5. Get a really good entry-level job.
6. Get promoted.
7. Get yourself into a serious, long-term relationship.
8. Get promoted.
9. Get married.
10. Get promoted.
11. Buy a house.
12. Get promoted.
13. Have children.
14. Get promoted a couple of more times.
15. Retire.
16. Ensure that your children do the same thing.

This list pushes far too many people to treat life as if it's a game: some sort of giant scavenger hunt in which we're all handed that list at the very beginning and told "check off as many things on this list as you can, as quickly as you can, because you're competing with everyone else to do it."

I was good at that game, but playing it almost destroyed

me. Adults told me I had the ability to absolutely rip through the list, so I assumed that's what they expected from me. Living up to that expectation is what drove me. After all, is there a feeling worse than letting down the people who have supported and believed in you?

Something on that list was supposed to be checked off by my twenty-fifth birthday. I don't remember what it was, but I do remember being irrationally upset about failing to achieve it. Suddenly, I had a terrifying but liberating moment in life. I realized a list was driving my life, impacting my decisions, and fueling my self-worth...and I hadn't written it. It was someone else's list. I was living my life according to someone else's agenda and I had to have the courage to stop.

I don't know what your list is. I have no way of knowing what list of things you feel you must check off to believe your life is a success and that you are a person of worth in this world. I do know that it's imperative that whatever that list is, *you* wrote it. It cannot be your parents' or your spouse's list, or crafted from your perception of what society expects from you, because if you spend your life chasing a list of other people's goals, you will always feel unfulfilled.

I admire Alison Ellwood because she had the courage to keep making changes in her life until it was the life she wanted and the life she deserved. You have the right to do that as well. In fact, you have an obligation to do so. Doing so means making courage a fundamental part of your daily life. You must be willing to deviate from the expectations of others when those expectations fail to live up to your own core values.

Be prepared though: the list and its expectations are tremendously powerful. They will often push us to violate our values in the name of checking the next thing off the list. They push us to make decisions based not on our core values but on what will best keep us moving through the list. Why the blind adherence to a template we didn't create? It's because the list becomes embedded as we grow up. Our education system is one of the most essential and empowering systems in our culture, but it can also be one of the most dangerous and oppressive because it doesn't teach courage—it teaches compliance. We need to change that, and we need to overcome the fact that it's something to which many of us have already fallen victim. I say this not as an indictment of teachers but to point out that the system in which they work often rewards seeking external validation more than it does seeking personal validation.

Every year thousands of young people are told the same thing: *if you just work hard enough, it will all pay off in the end.* The problem is we never tell them how hard is hard enough. We do a lousy job helping them figure out what they truly want the payoff in their life to be, and we never tell them when "the end" will come.

If you just work hard enough, it will all pay off in the end.

That statement makes young people believe that what their teachers think of them and what their employers think of them is somehow more important than what they think of themselves. It makes young people believe that the entire purpose of education is to figure out what the market wants, learn it, and then turn around and offer it right back to the market, regardless of whether it has anything to do with their skills, their gifts, or their passions.

Worst of all, it too often tells the dancers, the actors, the artists, the musicians, the entrepreneurs, the change agents, and anyone whose brilliance cannot be measured on essays and tests that their gifts aren't gifts at all: they're only gifts if one day they can be monetized, otherwise they should just be hobbies. Each one of us were once those young people. Some of you are experiencing it right now.

How old are some kids before they start to internalize that what they love to do, what makes them feel alive, and what they can create with their gifts won't move them through the list and won't reward them with the title of "leader"? Seven years old? Maybe eight? How different would our world be if we stopped doing that to eight-year-olds?

There are four essential truths about education I believe students should embrace on Day One. If you're a parent or a student reading this, I hope you choose to have the courage to make them a fundamental part of your approach to education.

1. You are far more brilliant than you give yourself credit for, and you are far more brilliant than any test will ever allow you to show.
2. School is the only time in your life when the ability to do well on a test is valued more than the ability to do something, change something, or help someone. There are so many more rewards in this world for being able to do, change, or help

than there are for writing tests. Make your education about developing your capacity to do things, change things, and help others as much as it is about writing tests, because one day we'll stop giving them to you.

3. Success and leadership cannot be measured by job titles or by paychecks and straight As will not get you on a direct path to either of those two things. Success and leadership come from striving to act, each day, in a way that makes it more likely you will add value to your own life and to the lives of others.

4. You should work incredibly hard to make your grades extraordinary. Your grades will open doors for you. Your grades will kick down doors for you. Your transcript is an incredibly important part of your life, but it is not a measure of your worth as a human being. If you are a C student, you are not a C person. If you are an A student, you are not automatically an A person. Never allow someone you know is a person of worth to think less of themselves because of numbers or letters handed out by someone else. The bottom line is this: *You should work incredibly hard to make your grades extraordinary, but you should work twice as hard to make sure they are the least impressive thing about you.*

Leadership is making your life less about living up to the expectations of others and more about a disciplined commitment to acting on your core values each day. Doing so risks loss: of money, of opportunities, of accolades, and potentially the respect of people whose admiration you've been taught to seek. However, it creates a repeated pattern of behavior of which you are proud in the long run. If the values you choose and the questions you create drive behavior that makes your life and the lives of the people around you better, those potential losses are almost always outnumbered by gains in internal pride and external respect.

Change Is Courage

It takes courage to look at your daily behaviors and ask, "Am I living up to what's important to me, or trying to satisfy a list of requirements for my life that have been imposed on me?"

It takes courage because discovering that your behaviors aim to keep you on path you didn't choose can be a shock. It causes you to start looking back and lament what has been and puts you face-to-face with a realization that most of us find unpleasant at best, terrifying at worst: I have to change.

I've met quite a few people who say they like change but significantly fewer who actually live like they do. Avoiding change is a natural human instinct. While the human brain is capable of remarkable feats, at its core it has one fundamental goal: keep us alive. Before the wonders of music, art, mathematics, and philosophy are possible, the people who create them must keep their hearts beating. As such our brains push us to seek safety, and if possible, safety on steroids: comfort.

An aversion to change once we have achieved a level of

comfort is of evolutionary benefit, and as such has become ingrained in our lives. Think about it: every one of us is the son or daughter, grandson or granddaughter, great-grandson or great-granddaughter (and so on) of people who survived. They've passed on the behavioral tendencies that helped them do so.

For most of human history, the primary threats to human survival were physical: we might starve, freeze to death, become infected with disease, be eaten, or otherwise succumb to threats in the physical environment in which we lived. So, we developed emotions—instincts that hijack rational thought and make us act without thinking. While acting without thinking is less than desirable today, rational thought is significantly slower than survival-based instinctive behavior, so we have a lot more survival-based instinctive behavior baked into our DNA than a tendency for rational thought.[5]

To illustrate what I mean, imagine two *homo erectus* wandering the savannah 100,000 years ago when a hungry lioness suddenly jumps out of the grass. One of the two has an immediate, instinctive reaction of fear, turns, and has run two steps before the thought "Argh! Lion!" even manages to make it into her brain.

The other thinks to himself, "Oh! A lioness! What are some of my options for survival here?"

The woman running through the tall grass screaming might be your many-times-over great-grandmother. The guy pondering his options? Probably not.

Our emotions exist because for most of human history they

made survival more likely. Anger, jealousy, fear, pride, and disgust all drive behavior that makes it more likely the person expressing them (and that person's genes) will live on. In the process they often caused tremendous pain, damage, and even death, but that wasn't always such a big deal in human society—however, it is now.

If you're able to buy and read this book you're probably privileged enough to no longer be living in a world where the primary threats to your survival are physical; you're living in a world where the primary threats with which you deal are social and emotional. In a world such as that, allowing your emotions to hijack your behavior is not an advantage. On the contrary, it will often lead to lost jobs, crumbling relationships, and a lack of trust and respect. Unfortunately, evolutionary changes in physiology and instinctive behavior occur much more slowly than shifts in social norms and expectations. Our brains are in many ways now forced to live in a world for which they are tremendously maladapted. In a world of skyscrapers, air travel that is statistically incredibly safe, and a wondrous variety of available foods, our brains still scream at us:

"Do NOT go up that high!"
"You're going WAY too fast right now!"
"This tastes wrong, spit it out!"

Too often our brains react to the person who sits across the conference table and challenges our idea the same way it would to the lioness that jumps from the grass: we either turn and flee or immediately counterattack. This stands in the way of true communication and collaboration.

I have a successful career as a speaker, and while I like to think much of that comes from an effort to hone my craft, I can't deny that part of the demand for my services comes from the fact that relatively few people are strong public speakers. In fact, a huge number of people are *terrified* of it. This makes sense: for most of human history being alone, undefended, and stared at by a large number of people was a tremendously dangerous situation. As such, those who tended to avoid it were more likely to have children and pass along that fear. Who knew that they'd be saddling their ancestors with a maladaptive fear in a world that rewards those who can fearlessly and charismatically deliver ideas in front of a group?

We're privileged to live in a world where many of the things that threatened our ancestors no longer pose a significant threat. However, we continue to carry the emotions and survival instincts of those ancestors to this day. Those instincts push us to be risk-averse when what is really required to thrive today is courage. They sound alarms about potential losses that long ago were mitigated for most people. Our DNA carries a message that used to keep us alive and now often keeps us from living: *"Where you are and what you are doing is keeping you sheltered, clothed, fed, and connected to other people. Stay put and keep doing those things. Do not change anything, because you have what you need and changing something might cause it to go away."*

Layered on top of this primal, evolutionary push away from change is a social stigma: change has been equated with failure. If you're changing something, the assumption is you failed at whatever it was you were doing before. Why would there be a need for change if what you were doing before wasn't somehow inadequate?

We must shake the idea that we begin our lives with a grade of 100 percent and each mistake we make along the way loses us points we can never earn back. That mindset makes us focus not on growing and learning through experimentation but on losing as few points as possible. We need to judge ourselves and each other by how wise and talented we are at this moment, not by how few mistakes we make along the way. Great learning happens through experimentation and iteration, and there can be no real experimentation without mistakes and failure.

Granted, change is not entirely stigmatized in our society: it's often celebrated as courage *after the fact* if it turns out the change was beneficial. However, change is treated as a limited resource: something that you should be willing to access, but not too often.

One way to understand the prevailing social perspective on change is to imagine you're given a stack of ten "change tokens" on Day One. Each one of these tokens represents a major change in your life. Whenever you undertake some sort of change you're required to turn in one of your tokens. More importantly, there is a socially acceptable pace at which these tokens can be utilized:

- You can turn in five by the time you're twenty-five.
- You can turn in three more by the time you're thirty.
- You can use the last two sometime between the ages of thirty and thirty-five.

Once you're out of change tokens—or if you try to turn one in past the age of thirty-five—well, clearly you don't have your act together, can't commit, and can't settle down. The implicit message is this: change too much or change too late, you're going to be judged, and not in a positive way.

What does that say to people who find themselves no longer in love after twenty-five years of marriage? Or in a job they no longer find rewarding (and perhaps never did)? Or who discover a new passion at forty they never knew existed? This is why courage needs to be a part of every leader's life on Day One: making courage part of your personal culture means you are always willing to keep making changes in your life until it is the life that you want and the life that you deserve. Courage in your life means you accept that there will be missteps—that constant and repeated change may be necessary, but that it is nothing to be ashamed of if it leads to a more fulfilling, positive outcome.

This culturally created schedule for change in our lives makes far too many leaders willing to settle short of the life they want and the life they deserve. It can be hard to detect when that's the case and tremendously upsetting once you do. As such, one of the most courageous questions anyone can ask is: *Where in my life am I settling?*

Where are you settling? In your career? In your relationships? In your health? It can be hard to recognize when you're settling, especially if you've achieved some level of objective success. I certainly have personal experience with that realization.

Too Young to Settle

A few years back, I found myself overloaded at work: eighteen-hour days, dealing with a difficult interpersonal conflict in my professional life, and completely burned out. As more and more of these days were strung together I couldn't ignore the fact I was acting less and less like the man I wanted to be. I was doing work begrudgingly instead of with passion, focusing on problems instead of solutions, and generally escalating situations instead of elevating them.

My tank was empty, and I knew it. Recognizing I was likely doing more harm than good at work, I arranged for some time off and decided to do something about which I had long dreamed: ride the train across Canada and back. While I intended the trip to be a quiet, reflective two weeks, it turned into one of the most dynamic and enlightening periods of my life, exposing me to teachers and insights I treasure to this day: you'll hear from a number of them in the coming pages. One was a young engineer named Caileigh.

I've always had a tremendous admiration for engineers. Their ability to pull apart problems and their commitment to the exploration of multiple possible solutions are skills I've tried to emulate in numerous leadership roles. Of course, they can also actually *build* things—a talent that has always escaped me. Throughout my youth, whenever the tools would come out and I'd ask, "How can I help?," the answer would inevitably be: "Don't touch anything!" It's humbling knowing that the best help you can provide is to do nothing. There's a leadership lesson in there somewhere.

I'm in awe of people whose minds are able to pick things

apart the way my engineer friends can. People who can apply fixed truths and unbendable laws to make flexible, creative—even artistic—solutions to seemingly impossible challenges. Which makes it not all that surprising that it was an engineer who first opened my eyes to the fact I was settling and who reminded me it was time to inject more courage into my life.

I met Caileigh on the third day of my trip. When I asked her where she was heading she blushed immediately, then sat back in her seat and looked at me as if considering whether I deserved to hear her story.

Finally, she said, "Okay, but before I tell you where I'm going and why, I need to tell you a story."

"Stories are my thing," I said.

"Well," she said. "This one's a love story. An engineering love story."

"Ah!" I said. "Is it yours?"

"That comes next," she replied. "This one is the story of the Roeblings. You ever hear of them?"

"No," I said. "But my students have to explain everything pop culture–related to me these days."

She laughed out loud. "Well, these guys haven't been pop culture since the mid-1800s."

I was intrigued. "All right, let's hear it."

"Well," she said. "During my first year in engineering, a professor told us the story of the Roeblings. For some reason it really stuck with me. During the Civil War, one of the best engineers in the world was a guy named John Roebling. He built huge suspension bridges: bigger than any bridges that had ever been built before. After the war, he and his son came up with an incredible design for the biggest suspension bridge in the world. You know which one it was?"

"No idea!" I replied.

"The Brooklyn Bridge—linking Manhattan to Brooklyn. Getting it across the East River meant building a bridge 50 percent longer than any suspension bridge in history. But he and his son had come up with all these innovative designs and they went for it."

"Obviously it worked out!" I laughed.

"Well, not so much for them actually," she replied. "Even before they started building it John Roebling was killed in a freak accident at the river, and then his son Washington ended up getting the bends, which partially paralyzed him."

"How do you get the bends while building a bridge, doesn't that come from diving?" I asked.

"Usually, yeah," she said. "Because it's actually known as DCS or decompression sickness, which you usually only experience through diving. Its original name was actually 'caisson disease' because that's the name of the huge towers that are built underwater into the bedrock to hold up big bridges. When they first started building them they had no idea of the impact the pressure difference could have on workers and a lot of them died from the bends. Washington Roebling was almost one of them."

"So, where does the love story come in?" I asked.

"Well, that's just it," she said. "Washington Roebling was incapacitated to the point he couldn't directly oversee the project anymore, but his wife, Emily Roebling, actually ended up learning *everything* about building bridges. She was the only one who saw Washington, and she'd carry messages back and forth between him and the onsite engineers. Eventually she learned so much that people figure a lot of the big design decisions being made were actually hers. Which is pretty amazing because she wasn't *allowed* to officially study to be an engineer, it was all her and her husband learning, teaching, and working together."

"I had never heard that story before!" I said.

"Yeah, they even tried to pull her husband off the project as chief engineer when they realized how big a role she was playing, and she went to bat with politicians, funders, the American Society of Civil Engineers, everyone. This was twelve years into building—and she managed to keep both of them in charge of the project."

Caileigh leaned back and smiled. "She spent hours with him every day working on making that bridge a reality. She taught herself to be an engineer for the two of them and that bridge. She built the damn thing, and she was the first person to walk across it."

"Nice," I whistled. "You're right, that's the very definition of a true engineering love story."

"Damn right," she said. "And from the moment I heard it it's been the most inspiring thing in my life. I want to be that passionate about my work and about someone else at the same time."

"So, you've found your engineering love story?"

"Well," she said sheepishly. "That's what I'm doing on the train. I'm actually going all the way to Vancouver to see a guy."

"Oh great!" I said. "Your boyfriend?"

She blushed. "Well...sort of."

"Sounds like a good story!" I said encouragingly.

"I guess it is," she said, sitting back with a shake of her head. "The fact is, we've never actually met in person. I met him on the Internet." She cut me off with a wave of her hand before I could say anything. "I know, I know. Everyone thinks I'm nuts. But it's been three years now, and we talk every day. Phone, email, texts. We know everything about each other, and we're completely in love."

"Man, how have you gone so long without seeing each other?" I asked.

"Well," she said with a resigned smile, "we've got almost everything in common, including the fact that we're both *terrified* of flying. We're both engineers, we both have huge loans, we both have new careers, and with neither one of us having cars, the only way we were going to see each other is if one of us took the train all the way across the country. This is the first time either one of us has had the time or the money to make it happen."

She leaned forward and spoke with intensity. "Look, I don't know if everyone in the world is entitled to a love story, but I want one, and I'll do whatever I have to do to get it. A lot of people think that's nuts and I have to be okay with that."

"But let me ask you this, Drew," she said after a moment, "how far would you be willing to go for the *chance* to be happier?"

How far would you be willing to go for the chance *to be happier?*

It was one of those questions that grows more powerful the longer it is pondered. Long after Caileigh and I said good-bye, it stuck with me. In fact, I remember it kept me up most of the night.

As I rode through the Rockies that night, I realized I didn't like my answer. I had to acknowledge that *"I'm not willing to go very far at all for the chance to be happier."*

When I started my trip, I thought I had everything I was *supposed* to have to be happy: a good job, great job security, and a position at a prestigious university. My work had started to make me unhappy, tired, and bitter, but I figured it wasn't because something was missing; it was because I didn't *appreciate* what I had. Almost *everyone's* work made them unhappy, tired, and bitter I figured, and many of them didn't get the pay or the benefits I did, so who was I to complain? I just needed to find a way to appreciate my good fortune and ignore these "silly" feelings of unhappiness.

Caileigh's question brought me to a powerful realization: creating the chance to be happier meant making changes in my life, and I wasn't willing to make those changes if it meant risking what I already had. I drifted off to sleep feeling demoralized and more than a bit cowardly.

The next morning it struck me: I didn't really *like* what I already had! What I had may have looked great to others, but it made me feel okay at best as a person. I was willing to settle for okay rather than chase the possibility of being happier. I had never thought of myself as someone who would settle for okay, and it was a real shock to realize that's exactly what I had allowed myself to become. I quit my job and founded my company shortly after. I love the life I have now—and I take risks every day to keep it that way.

It's not possible to lead others if we're not willing to lead ourselves and a key step toward effective personal leadership is the willingness to honestly ask ourselves: "In what areas of my life am I settling?" Are you settling for okay in your job? In your relationships? In your health? In your level of hope and optimism? Leadership is having the courage to be honest with yourself about where in your life you are allowing yourself to settle and taking action to ensure you don't do it for a single day longer.

I don't care how old you are, you're simply too young to settle.

Five Ways You Can Embody *Courage* Today (on Day One)

1. Actively attempt to be rejected three times.
2. Sit down and consider what list you're using as the checklist for success in your life. Ask yourself, "Did I write this list?"
3. Do something that requires five seconds of extraordinary courage.
4. Ask yourself, "Where in my life am I settling?" Tell a friend your answer and ask them to hold you accountable for changing it.
5. Speak up in support of someone with an unpopular opinion you believe is right.

Questions You Can Ask to Operationalize *Courage*:

- What did I try today that might not work, but I tried it anyway?
- What did I do today that scared me?
- What did I do today that I wanted to avoid?
- What did I do today that I'm proud of myself for trying?

TEN

Empowerment

A commitment to acting as a catalyst for the success of others.

QUESTION: What have I done today to make it more likely someone else will move closer to a goal?

The Problem with Drew Dudley

I had just finished speaking at a major business school when a young man approached me and said, "Drew, I've seen you speak three times this year and I really like the stories that you tell."

I thanked him with a smile, which he repaid by asking, "Do you want to know what's wrong with you?"

Figuring you should never take a pass on having a complete stranger tell you what's wrong with you, I invited him to go ahead.

"You never tell anybody how to win," he said.

Confused, I asked him, "I'm sorry, win what?"

He rolled his eyes at me and in an exasperated tone said, "Come on, this is a game we're playing here. I've known that from the very first time that somebody gave me a grade. I mean, why would they be grading us and ranking us if wasn't to make sure that the people at the top got something the people at the bottom didn't get? There is only so much money and there are only so many jobs. If I don't get them somebody else will. You're not doing us any favors by telling us that there is some kinder reality out there. All you're doing is setting us up to get destroyed in the game. If you really want to help us, stop doing that and start telling us how to win."

With that, he walked off.

I was stunned, but he was right. Through all my presentations, I never spent any time telling anyone how to win that game. So here, for all of you, is how to win that game.

Don't play that game. There are no winners in that game. There are only people who have been beaten. Viewing life as a game with winners and losers leads us to believe that we operate in an economy of scarcity: where anything you get leaves a little less for me. That perception is the source of so many of the things of which we are ashamed in our society: greed, jealousy, the building of empires on the exploitation of others, and the bullying that begins on our playgrounds and continues up into our boardrooms.

Leaders choose to live in a different type of economy: an economy of abundance.[6] In an economy of scarcity the focus is always on profit. In an economy of abundance the focus is always on value. Leaders seek value, not profit.

An economy of abundance acknowledges there are only so many jobs and there is only so much money out there, but embraces the belief that there is no limit to the amount of satisfaction available to us, no limit to the amount of self-worth available to us, and no limit to the amount of happiness available to us if we are able to separate satisfaction, self-worth, and happiness from our paychecks and from our job titles.

An economy of abundance dismisses the idea that "the secret to happiness is freedom, and the secret to freedom is money." That belief has taught generations of people to chase money and jobs as the primary goals in their lives. I was one of them, I was good at it, and I was tremendously unhappy. I would go to work every day aiming to impress someone I worked for in the hopes they would give me my life goals. *I hoped someone* else *would deliver my life goals.* To live in an economy of abundance, you must accept that money and jobs make lousy life goals because you're not in charge of either one.

How hard you work and how well you work will always play a role in how much money you make. However, as long as you work for someone else (and let's face it most of us will spend most of our lives working for somebody else), how much money you make is *someone else's* decision. If you get promoted, are given more responsibility or a bigger job title, it is because *someone else* has the power to give you those things. If you receive an award or are recognized in any other way for your work, it is because *someone else* has the power to give that to you.

Tying our fundamental life goals to someone else's whims is tremendously disempowering. One of the reasons so few people put up their hand when asked if they are a leader is they've accepted a situation where the things that they are chasing in their life—the things they believe will make them happy—can only come from someone else. It's hard to feel like a leader living in that reality, but you don't need to quit your job, sell your house, and seek spiritual enlightenment somewhere to change it.

Here's the Part Where I Use a Buzz Term

My life in an economy of abundance and accompanying personal, financial, and business success began when I said to myself, "I will no longer chase goals in my life that can only be delivered by others." My life in an economy of abundance started when I shifted to a single goal over which I was entirely responsible: *I will try to* add tremendous value *in every single interpersonal interaction of which I am part.*

"Add value" is the two-word advice I share all over the world with anyone willing to listen or who must sit through my speech to get a free meal at a conference. Adding value is the key to living in an economy of abundance. It is the key to successful careers and relationships. It is the key to creating more leaders and more people who feel comfortable calling themselves leaders.

Feel free to roll your eyes. I recognize that "add value" has become as much a buzz term as "synergy," "personal brand," or "gameify." I spent many an hour trying to create my own version of the term. The thing is, the term really is on point, so I'll aim to explain what it means to me specifically.

In this context, adding value means trying to find a way to give someone something they didn't know they needed and didn't know they wanted in every interaction. It means aiming to develop skills and insights with the intention of being able to offer greater resources and support to the efforts of others. This is a departure from our instinct to "figure out what the person at the front of the room wants and give it to them." That behavior is rewarded after all: dedicate your life to figuring out what that teacher, professor, or boss wants and deliver it to them and you will have a comfortable life. You're never going to thrive, however; you're never going to be free and you're never going to lead. Those things come from seeking to give people things they didn't know they wanted.

Adding value means no longer asking, "What do I have to do to get a great job" or "What do I have to do to shine brighter than everyone around me?" Adding value means asking, "How do I become someone who is *great* at jobs?" and "Who do I need to be to make everyone around me shine even brighter?"

When you ask, "What do I have to do?" your focus is on pleasing other people. Asking "Who do I need to be?" shifts focus to what you expect from yourself. That represents a fundamental change in your understanding of who ultimately needs to be satisfied with your life.

Leaders don't treat jobs and money as goals in and of themselves. Instead, they accept that jobs and money are the natural by-products that come to anyone who adds tremendous value. It is far better to put your energy, time, and focus into figuring out how you can add tremendous value rather than how you can make money and get jobs. It takes a leap of faith to make that shift in focus, but it is a leap that has paid off for me in every way imaginable. That payoff is available to anyone willing to ask, "Are the goals I'm chasing in my life actually my goals, or are they the natural by-products that would come to me if I became better at adding value?"

Living in an economy of abundance and focusing on adding value does not mean you have to give up on dreams of business success or personal financial wealth. Living in an economy of abundance does not mean that you don't focus on profit (trust me, I focus on profit). It means you recognize that profit is only one type of value, and whoever adds the most value will inevitably reap the biggest profits: not just financially, but emotionally, socially, physically, and spiritually as well.

You may not realize it, but every single night our brain checks in with us about our goals. If your goal is money, every single night your brain will ask, "Hey, am I rich?"

If your goal is prestigious job titles, every single night your brain will ask, "Hey, did I get promoted today?"

If your goal is to outshine everyone else, every night your brain will ask, "Does everyone recognize me as the absolute best at what I do?"

For most of us the answer to at least two of those questions will be no almost every night. If your mind tells you that you haven't reached your goals day after day, it changes you: you become bitter, cynical, and angry. It turns you into someone who is less capable of adding value and therefore gets fewer of the things that you want.

Give yourself only one goal—to add tremendous value in every interpersonal interaction of which you are part—and each night your answer to "Did I add value today?" becomes: "Yes. Just like yesterday, and just like the day before that." (At least if you apply the process laid out in this book!)

Acknowledging you accomplished your primary goal every night changes the way you feel about yourself and it changes the way you interact with others. It makes you capable of adding even more value and getting even more of the things that you want out of life. It turns you into someone who leads every day.

This may sound unrealistically altruistic (it's not unrealistic, it's hard—don't confuse the two) but it is not an entirely selfless process. Being recognized as someone who empowers others comes with inevitable personal and professional benefits.

During a Q&A session at another business school, one of the professors asked me to identify "the single most transformative moment" in my career. It was a question that I had never considered, and I took so long to come up with an answer that the silence got to be a little embarrassing for all of us. Finally, I realized the truth.

"You know what?" I said finally. "I probably wasn't in the room for the most transformative moment in my career."

I can't identify the single most transformative moment in my career, but there's a pretty good chance it was a moment when a group of people in a meeting to which I wasn't invited decided to provide me with an opportunity. Perhaps it was the group who chose to offer me admission to the university where I met so many of the people who shaped my way of thinking. Perhaps it was the group who decided to select me as the person to build their (and my) first leadership development program. Perhaps it was the group who chose to give me the opportunity to share my story of the lollipop moment at TEDxToronto, or the group that chose to take the video of that talk and place it on one of the world's most popular websites. Our access to some opportunities in life is controlled by others, so perhaps it's best to make our lives about empowering others. People remember who helped move them forward.

The key is to no longer try to outperform others but rather to become indispensable. If you have a skill or develop a skill that allows you to outperform 90 percent of the people in an organization, you're probably going to make six figures. However, if you can become the type of person who makes everyone who works with you outperform everyone who doesn't work with you, you become indispensable.

How do you become indispensable? What kind of question can help ensure you do at least one thing each day to help empower others? For me, the answer came from behind the wheel of a cab.

Turn In Your Service

Horus had spent twenty-seven years as a teacher before becoming a driver. Perhaps that's why he seemed so eager to share a lesson as we headed toward the French Quarter in New Orleans.

"When we went to war in Iraq the first time," he began, "I remember picking up *USA Today* one morning and reading the story about a young man killed in action. They mentioned that he had inscribed something into the back of his dog tags: Joshua 1:9.

"Do you know the story of Joshua?" he asked me.

"I may have once, but I've no doubt forgotten," I replied.

"Well, to make a long story very short," he said, "Joshua was made the leader of his people, and he was challenged by God to do a lot of things that seemed impossible—beyond his ability as a single man, or honestly, seemingly beyond the abilities of all of his people together. But whenever he had the courage to trust that greatness was possible, great things happened."

"What is that particular biblical passage, Joshua 1:9?" I asked.

"Have I not commanded you? Be strong and courageous. Do not be afraid; do not be discouraged, for the Lord your God will be with you wherever you go," Horus answered instantly.

"So, what's my advice?" he asked, glancing back in the mirror. "Do not be afraid of your greatness. But know that individually we are limited, collectively we are limitless. When we share with each other, we increase our capacity to give.

"Now," he continued, "too many people don't share with one another because they think there's only so much out there and they think that they need to collect as much as they can for themselves before someone else gets it. They think to reach greatness they have to accumulate as much as they can until they feel that nothing is missing in their lives. So many people think they aren't great because something is 'missing.' So, they search for it, grabbing what they can from others in case that's the thing that's missing in their life.

"But here's the thing," he said, turning slightly so he could look at me out of the corner of his eye. "In your life right now, in this world right now, everything is available. Nothing is missing. You have everything you need for greatness, so you must live, and live now.

"If you don't live with all you have right now, you'll never earn or be given more. You can't be inert and wait to seize your greatness because something is missing. Live with everything you've got every day because it's the only way what you've got will grow."

He paused for a moment before continuing.

"Drew, you are destined for greatness. We are all destined for greatness. Your greatness is waiting to be claimed. But like anything that you want to claim, you have to turn something in to get it."

He gave me one final look as we pulled into the hotel.

"Drew, what you have to turn in for your greatness is service. Turn in your service, get your greatness."

"What do you mean by 'turn in your service'?" I asked.

"We serve others whenever we help them move closer to one of their goals," he responded. "For some people that might mean an educational goal, a career goal, or a goal related to their legacy. But let me tell you, the most important goals you can help someone reach are the goals related to their dignity. People need to feel seen, they need to feel understood, they need to feel connected to another person. Too many people in this world don't have those goals met."

He popped out of the car and hustled around to open my door. As I stepped out he grasped my hand and finished his thought.

"If you want to turn in your service, Drew, help someone reach a goal. And if ever you don't know how, just take a moment to see someone, listen to someone, or connect with someone."

And with that, I was enveloped in a big bear hug.

On that day, my Day One question for living the value of empowerment was born:

What have I done today to make it more likely someone else will move closer to a goal?

Five Ways You Can Embody *Empowerment* Today (on Day One)

1. Ask yourself, "What do I wish someone had done to help me earlier in my life/career?" Go do that thing for someone else.
2. Pick someone in your LinkedIn network and provide an endorsement.
3. Donate $5 to a random Kickstarter or GoFundMe campaign.
4. Say something positive about someone who isn't in the room. Make sure their boss, colleague, or someone of influence hears you.
5. Be a "friendtor"—someone who tells tough truths to make their friends better.

Questions You Can Ask to Operationalize *Empowerment*:

- What did I do today to move someone else closer to a goal?
- How did I make someone stronger today?
- How did I turn in my service today?
- What did I do today to make someone shine brighter?

ELEVEN

Growth

A commitment to expanding the capacity to add value.

QUESTION: What did I do today to make it more likely someone would learn something?

Empowerment vs. Growth

If the value of empowerment is personally adding value to others, the value of growth is about becoming better at doing just that.

Growth is an expansion in the capacity to add value. You embody it any time you aim to increase someone's ability to improve, yourself included. You embody growth any time you act as a catalyst for learning, any time you can answer the question: *What have I done today to make it more likely someone will learn something?*

When we're children growth happens rapidly with very little conscious action on our part. We picked up language and social norms without consciously saying to ourselves, "I'll be spending the rest of my life in this society, better do some research on how that's done," and you found yourself getting a little taller as the years went on without doing anything specific to make it happen. When we're young, growth just happens.

As we get older maintaining a healthy pace of growth takes conscious planning and effort. It becomes all too easy to fill our lives with things that keep us busy but don't keep us growing. Go too long without appreciable growth in your life and not only does it become difficult to see yourself as a leader, it becomes difficult to feel like you matter. My growth-driving question was born during my first face-to-face encounter with that reality: at the start of my transformative train ride ten years ago.

"Don't All Books Have Stories?"

When I started out, I didn't want to talk to anyone the entire two weeks I was on that train. Work had broken me, and my only desire was to escape into the tiny world of my sleeper car and sever all human connections. I told myself it would be the perfect opportunity to read the pile of books and articles I had shamefully been keeping on the back burner.

Not long after departing I moved to the lounge car at the very back of the train. I was pleased to find it deserted and settled in to begin my reading. A few minutes later a young girl of perhaps seven or eight burst into the lounge and began circling the car, arms outstretched like an airplane. With her bright yellow top and black pants, she resembled some sort of giant grinning bumblebee. After perhaps three tours around the space, she dipped back out through the entrance and was gone.

Ten minutes later she was back, taking three silent rotations around the car before disappearing out the door once again. Eventually I realized this young girl was doing "laps" of the train: running up and down the center aisle from car to car, front to back, over and over again. Finally, after three or four trips, she plopped down in the seat next to me. No one else in the car and she chose to sit right next to me. This threw me off a little as at the time I had very little experience talking to children. I don't have any of my own and neither do most of my closest friends. It's not that I don't like children, it's that I'm kind of terrified of screwing them up. Yet here was this little girl, smiling and swinging her legs off the edge of the seat right next to me.

"Hello!" she said brightly. "My name is Allison! What's yours?"

"Hello, Allison," I said with only a slight glance up from my book, trying to politely convey the fact I really didn't wish to speak to anyone. "My name is Drew."

"What are you reading?" she asked, completely undeterred.

"Oh, just a book for work," I replied.

Her eyes spread wide. "You get to *read books* for work?" she asked incredulously. "My dad has to go to an office!"

I couldn't help but laugh. "Well yes," I said, "I guess I do get to read for work!"

"You're really lucky," she smiled. "I love to read. What's the story of your book?"

"Oh," I said, looking down half-ashamed at the dry,

theory-heavy tome in my hand. "I guess this book doesn't really *have* a story."

"Don't all books have stories?" she asked quizzically.

"Well no," I replied. "Some just have…knowledge, I guess."

She tilted her head at me. "Aren't stories knowledge?"

It was here my insecurity about talking to kids bubbled to the surface. I wasn't going to send this perfectly nice young girl away having taught her stories were not in fact knowledge!

"Oh, for sure!" I sputtered, stumbling to recover. "In fact, I once met a brilliant man who told me that 'the story is the basic unit of human understanding.' "[7]

As soon as it was out of my mouth I felt like an idiot. This girl was maybe eight years old; surely "the story is the basic unit of human understanding" was a concept a tad too advanced to be dropping on her.

Allison just looked thoughtful for a moment. Finally, she looked up and with a self-assured nod informed me: "I think your friend is very smart."

I couldn't help but laugh. I hadn't seen such confidence and poise in someone so young before.

"I think you're right!" I said with a grin. "But can I ask you something, Allison? Why have you been running up and down the train?"

"Oh," said Allison, seeming almost disappointed that I hadn't asked her something more challenging. "I'm running to remind myself."

"Remind yourself of what?" I asked.

"Well," she said, "my parents say that I have a very big spirit. In fact, they say that my spirit is too big for basically every room that I'm in."

"All right," I said. "I've met a lot of people like that. They make really good friends."

She smiled. "Well, you know how a train is kind of like a big long hallway?"

"Well...yes, I guess so!" I replied.

"Well, if my spirit is too big for rooms, it is definitely too big for hallways," explained Allison. "And anytime I'm stuck somewhere that isn't big enough to fit my spirit, I run. I run to remind myself that I'm always free if I want to be."

The matter-of-fact way she said "I'm always free if I want to be" had a profound impact on me in that moment: when was the last time I had reveled in my freedom or acted to remind myself that my life was ultimately mine to control? When had I forgotten that while I often couldn't control what I had to do every day I was always in charge of who I was? With a single sentence Allison reminded me of the man I could be at both work and play: passionate, outgoing, and full of life. I also realized I wasn't being that man anymore, and ultimately that was my choice.

"You know what, Allison?" I said with a smile. "I honestly haven't been feeling so great lately, and what you just said makes me really happy. It makes me think that maybe that's what's been bothering me: that my spirit is just too big for the places I'm spending my time."

Allison hopped off the seat and looked at me for a moment, almost professorially to be honest. Then slowly, as if choosing her words carefully, she said, "Drew, I do not mean to be rude, but I don't think anyone whose spirit is too big for hallways would ever read a book without a good story."

With that she smiled, spread her arms wide, spun three times around the car, and was gone.

I don't know the key to happiness, but unhappiness is inevitable when you allow a gap to form between your conception of who you are and how you behave. In those few words Allison had made me aware of that gap in my life. I had always thought of myself as someone who could connect with others and add value; someone who seized every opportunity to learn and try new things; someone who would never let life just pass him by.

Yet I had booked a single sleeper car. I had been happy to find the lounge car deserted. My plan heading into the trip was to *avoid* talking to others and bury my head in books. My identity was someone who gathered and shared stories and insights and yet I was going to spend a month of my life not only avoiding books with a good story but avoiding stories entirely. The behaviors of the man in my head could not have been more different than the behaviors of the man on that train.

Leaders come in many forms, and it was a tiny one who showed me that if I really wanted to "recharge" on the trip, I needed to reengage with who I wanted to be. I had to close the gap between the identity I believed in and how I was acting.

So, for the rest of that trip I was "that guy" on the train: the one who sat down unannounced and asked to hear your story. The one who sat with strangers at meals, bought drinks in the lounge car, and believed that everyone had a story that would teach me something. That day I began asking the first iteration of my Day One question tied to growth: *What have I done today to make it more likely I will learn something?* Later that night it taught me my first lesson.

One Day vs. Next-Day Leadership

"Thirty-five years he worked to get away from the office, and now he can't stop talking about it," Camille said in a mock angry tone.

I was back in the lounge car a few hours later, having a drink with Camille and her husband, Albert. While I was making the trip at the age of thirty-two, Albert and Camille had been putting it off for almost that long. Albert had started a public relations company in his late twenties and building, growing, and maintaining it had eaten up more than three decades. They wasted no time after his retirement, however: less than a week had passed since his final day at the office and they were already three days into their long-awaited trip.

Inspired by my interaction with Allison, I'd bought a couple glasses of wine, introduced myself, and asked if I could join them. It wasn't long before Albert was sharing stories of his time as president and CEO, and before we knew it two hours had flown by, prompting Camille's gentle reminder that perhaps a change of subject was in order.

"All right, all right!" I laughed. "One more question and then nothing more about work."

Camille shot me a fake stink eye, then nodded her agreement with a poorly concealed smile.

"What's the most important leadership lesson you took away from all of those years?" I asked Albert.

"I learned the 'two days of leadership,'" he replied.

My quizzical look led him to explain.

"I worked for thirty-five years in PR," he said. "And I came to realize that sometimes it was about building a brand and sometimes it was about saving a brand. When you're building a brand you have a plan, and for the most part you're in control of how and when it's executed, but there's always a crisis eventually. Someone does or says something stupid, or something fails that wasn't supposed to, or any one of a million things goes wrong to throw you into damage control. You can do your best to plan for those moments, but control is rarely in your hands once they start unfolding.

"Leadership is the same way," he continued. "I came to think of it as the 'two days of leadership': one-day leadership and next-day leadership."

"What's the difference?" I asked.

"'One-day' leadership is strategic leadership," he said. "It's the vision of where you want to be 'one day,' the timeline for when you want that day to arrive, and the creation of the plan to take you there."

"So, it's your vision and mission," I chimed in.

"Yes, plus the strategic objectives, timelines, measures, and targets you create to take you there," he said with a nod. "'Next-day leadership,' on the other hand, goes into action when crisis necessitates simplification. It means assessing a lot of information in a short time and quickly discarding the nonessential to get to the essential. It's letting go of the hope of achieving 'the best' and focusing on 'the best we can do at present.' That's where the name comes from: it's simply about getting you to the next day.

"Every successful organization and individual is good at next-day leadership," he continued. "You can get very good at dealing with things that way. So good in fact that it can become your default method of dealing with everything, and that's when organizations get themselves in trouble. Next-day leadership can't become your norm. 'Fast and simple' can't be your default position, no matter how effective you are at it. If you allow it to be your first option, all you ever focus on is getting through until tomorrow, and when tomorrow comes it's all about cleaning up the quick fixes and the ruffled feathers from yesterday."

Wanting to keep my promise to Camille, I thanked Albert and returned to my sleeper, his idea of the "days of leadership" bouncing around my head. He was right: we become proud of our ability to boil down, strip away, and "get it done" when crises call for it. However, seeing how effective it is we sometimes do it even in the absence of a crisis. We begin to lead on a need-to-know-only basis: "Just tell me what I have to know to get through this, I don't have time to deal with anything else."

You can't lead on a need-to-know-only basis. You can fix things, you can maintain, but you can't lead. The things you boil down and cut away during next-day leadership often provide the information needed for long-term positive change— the creation of which is what leadership is all about. If you cut them away every time and not just when crisis dictates, you're dooming yourself to an endless cycle of crises and very little growth. Next-day leadership is a crucial skill, but it's essential to check in and ensure you haven't let it become your default position.

I couldn't shake the feeling there was something missing from Albert's framework, however: an understanding of the power of *everyday leadership*. At lunch the next day I sat down and shared the story of the "lollipop moment" and how it had helped me redefine leadership as a focus on creating daily positive interpersonal impact. I asked him if there was a place for that concept of leadership in a business world that was often all about the bottom line and could often be cutthroat.

"Absolutely," he replied. "I think the key to real productivity is making clear to others that you want to have a positive impact on their lives and that you're willing to work to do so. Most of my staff weren't trying to *take* my job, but they did want to *get* my job one day. I didn't see that as a threat. I think the best thing I did for my company was to try to let everyone who worked for me know I cared about their development the same way I cared about my own. I didn't want an environment where I had a bunch of people who would 'one day' be able to take over for me. I wanted a company where I knew I had a bunch of people who could take over for me tomorrow, because one day that was going to be the reality."

A key facet of leadership is figuring out how to send Albert's message every day: you're as interested in the development of the people around you as you are your own. It's not enough to be supportive when you see opportunities to help people, you must be a catalyst for creating those opportunities and for giving others the tools to create them for themselves.

There are all kinds of books and all kinds of speakers on

how to build better teams. In my experience that takes care of itself when your mission is to create better team members and better teammates. Forget power, influence, and control: make people feel like they're better when you're around and they will follow you anywhere.

In those first few days after my interaction with Allison, I sought out the stories of as many people as I could. I was traveling in the first-class section of the train, however, and with most of the passengers being quite well off the insights often resembled Albert's: stories pulled from experiences leading organizations and building businesses. My experience on the train was a microcosm of how leadership insights are gathered more broadly: from those with money, titles, prestige, and influence. That is certainly a *form* of leadership, but as I hope you've gathered by now it's crucial we recognize that's not where the definition of leadership ends—a fact hammered home by a bartender named Patty.

Why Are You on the Train?

A couple of days after my conversation with Albert, I entered the bar car, ordered a drink from Patty, and settled into what had become my usual seat. Patty approached a few moments later with my drink and asked, "Drew, do you mind if I answer a question you didn't ask me?"

Confused, I asked, "What do you mean?"

She smiled and with a little bit of embarrassment said, "Well, it's hard not to overhear conversations in here, and I hope you don't mind, but I've found the conversations you've been having with people over the past few days really interesting so I've kind of been listening in."

"I don't mind at all," I laughed. "In fact, I feel lucky that *I've* had the chance to listen in!"

"Well," she said, "whoever you've been talking with, at some point you ask them what they think is the most important thing they had learned in their life. I don't know why but I haven't been able to get that question out of my mind, and I've been sort of working on my own answer. I know I'm just a bartender, but I was wondering if I could tell you what I came up with?"

At that point I wasn't yet on the lookout for "just," so I recognize I missed an opportunity for leadership when I simply said, "Of course, I'd love to hear it!"

Patty did a quick glance at the other patrons before placing my drink on the table and sitting down next to me.

"Well, first let me ask you this: why are you on this trip?"

"What do you mean?" I asked.

"There are a lot of much faster, less expensive ways to get around than the train, so why are you on this trip?"

"Oh," I replied. "I'm heading all the way across Canada. It's something I've always wanted to do."

Patty smiled.

"I've been on this job for twenty-three years and I've discovered you can learn so much about someone by how they answer the question, 'Why are you on this trip?' The richest people tell me exactly where they're going. The most interesting people tell me where they've been. The happiest? They just tell me what direction they're headed.

"So, the most important thing I've learned?" she continued. "The key to getting the most out of life is understanding each of three crucial things: where exactly you want to get, what direction you need to go to get there, and what stops you need to hit along the way.

"You know what's funny?" she commented as she stood up and headed back toward the bar. "I've always known that, but until I heard you ask, 'What's the most important thing you've learned,' I never realized I knew it."

She gave a big laugh. "I feel bad I never told my kids!"

"Until I heard you ask . . . I never realized I knew it."

Two things changed with her statement. First, my growth-driving question evolved just a little bit: "What did I do today to make it more likely I will learn something?" became "What have I done today to make it more likely *someone* would learn something?" Some days the growth can be your own, other days you can be the catalyst for growth in others. The key is that the value of growth is in some way embodied through the facilitation of learning.

Providing answers isn't always the best way to help someone learn: the right question can be an absolute gift. Craft your questions so that the very process of considering the question is a lesson in and of itself: where the pursuit of the answer, not necessarily the answer itself, will make the other person better. "Why do you matter" isn't intended to solicit an answer—it's intended to show people they *don't have* an answer. The learning happens in the follow-up questions they ask themselves about why that is.

Effective leaders don't have more answers than anyone else; they ask better questions and listen to more stories. The story is indeed the basic unit of human understanding, and we cannot expect to understand ourselves or each other if we're not willing to constantly hear new stories and tell our own. Yet so many of the people I meet are either unwilling or unable to tell their own stories. They believe them to be boring, stupid, or unimportant compared to the stories of others. Growing as a leader means accepting that your story matters and becoming conscious about what it might have to teach. The best way to learn something is to teach it, so if you want to better understand your own story, ask yourself: *"What can my story teach others?"*

The second change: when Patty told me, "Until I heard you ask, I never realized I knew," I became committed to creating a new leadership tool: a question that would draw out stories from others. A compelling question that would require the person being asked to search for and articulate wisdom they may not have realized they possessed. The right question would make me both a teacher and a learner each time I asked it, effectively answering my personal growth-driving question: "What did I do today to make it more likely someone would learn something?"

I realized the answer lay in Patty's final comment: "I feel bad I never told my kids."

And with that, the Edge of the Bed Question was born.

The Edge of the Bed Question

Imagine it's the final night your son or daughter is living in your house (this may require imagining you have a son or a daughter). Tomorrow they're off to school, getting married, or moving away to start their first job. You're walking by their room and they call you in. As you sit down on the edge of their bed, they look up at you and ask: "Mom/Dad, what's your best life advice? What single insight has most contributed to your happiness?"

What would you tell them? That's the Edge of the Bed Question.

The Edge of the Bed Question is my icebreaker. I use it to get people to start telling their stories. It's my attempt to gain insight for myself while helping others identify what their stories can teach others. I've asked it on planes, trains, and buses. Posed it to CEOs, children, and the homeless. It comes up at every dinner party and over pretty much every coffee date. It's a source of tremendous personal growth and a constant reminder that leadership insight comes from everywhere.

Asking the Edge of the Bed Question is an easy way for me to answer my Day One growth-related question. Remember: what sets great leaders apart isn't that they have all the answers, it's that they ask powerful questions where the person providing the answer learns just as much as the person asking the question. Some of the most inspiring leadership insights I've gained over the years have come from a question born from the mouth of a seven-year-old and refined by a bartender.

For many years it was a weekly feature on my website: people from all walks of life shared wisdom big and small, poignant and hilarious. I learned to "never try to throw out a used trash can," that it was important to "love being a grip," and to "always pack a bathing suit." Always buried beneath the silly titles were touching stories of love and vulnerability. Many of those I asked to make a submission no doubt saw it as an imposition at first, but not a single one failed to say thank you for the opportunity when they turned it in. They put their time and energy into writing a thousand words and ended up thanking me for it. That's the power of a question aimed at growth.

Seek to unlock the wisdom of others because in doing so you grow your own. Sometimes you'll be laid flat by what you hear—as I was when I received this Edge of the Bed submission from a singer, dancer, and bringer of joy named Steph Berntson:

Lessons from Alchemy

By Steph Berntson

From the Edge of the Bed Advice Series

I want to start with a little story about how I learned big truths from French people.

"In the face of an absurd universe—one lacking transcendent, factory-installed meanings—we are compelled to create our own." (Albert Camus, *La Peste*, 1947)

Six years ago, I went out to my local bar, Not My Dog, with my bacchanalian (then) manfriend. It was a grim Sunday evening: I had to haul out to a job I hated first thing the next morning and a stack of paperwork taunted me back home in the living room. I was expecting the worst kind of nothing from the world.

Thus, BEER.

Now, beer ain't a solution (well, literally it is, so think figuratively), but I was out to forget about the coming week. My daily routine felt tight and awkward right then. My laundry wasn't done. I was having trouble chatting nicely in public. I lost socks. I kept getting stuck on the subway. My haircut was, at best, a winter raccoon fight.

In the middle of my first pint, a pianist ambled up to the ad hoc stage unannounced (Not My Dog is always gig-ready). He was competent, but more than that, he exuded HAPPY. Primed for anything. His hair and glasses bounced and tilted with the kind of bumpy jouissance that reminds you of *The Muppet Show*. He rifled off some jazz. The manfriend and I pretended to scat. Whether on account of the felicity of (1) the good music or (2) the good beer, I relaxed.

Out of the little listening crowd, a thin, shaking woman shoots up and announces that she's finally ready to "try the song."

"NOW! I WANT TO TRY THE SONG NOW, TIM!"

The jazz piano man gapes, then thumps three times on his instrument. Morse code. She knocks back a full pint glass. Moving through the constellation of tiny tables, the mystery Ms. sings Barbara's "Gare de Lyon," a French tune from the 60s I've never heard before.

What happens then is a rare kind of Sunday alchemy: the room screech-halts and just listens.

The singer is nervous, but good—she growls perfect French gutturals through the whole damn melody. She looks transported. Then ecstatic. I don't think she IS a singer—she's just a moderate drinker and Francophile who's suddenly brave. I speak French, so the lyrics entreat me to get on a train and fall in love in another country. Transportational. The piano continues to rumble bass notes and "Viens—faire tes bagages, nous partons en voyage—" shivs the air. The singer gets bold and bolder. She's reached the piano in a tranced half-delirium, shining.

"VIENS ME DIRE 'JE T'AIME,' COMME TOUS CEUX QUI S'AIMENT—"

She's reached the stage. She smacks the piano body with her boot to finish—an exclamation mark. The pianist and singer breathe at each other. She beams. We're ALL ecstatic now. Who was this? Who booked this? Is this a gig night? Wha' just happened? Where did she come from? What is this song? Where are we? Can we still book tickets to Paris? You wanna fall in love? GARE DE LYON! How?

We clap. We HOLLER. YES! GARE DE LYON! GARE DE—!

The room settles. The pianist and singer nod at each other and drift. It's over. Something is over. Anti-alchemy: gold spins back into the two dull halves of Sunday evening.

I finish my beer. Drunk manfriend and I skip home. We scat, we speak French at the chain-link, we laugh. And there are three things I've learned in this accidental catechism:

1. **Let chaos in.** You know what life's like? Tap dancing. Adaptability is crucial. It's like good ole Albert Camus says: "Accepting the absurdity of everything around us is one step, a necessary experience: it should not become a dead end. It arouses a revolt that can become fruitful."

2. **Be emotionally generous to your absolute limit.**
Especially if you've had the benefit of a lot of privilege. Sympathy is a luxury. Empathy is a rare grab.
If you luck into either of these, revel in them. Think
of empathy like the fruitcake of the emotional spectrum: re-gift.

3. **Play never ever stops being relevant.** Embellish,
reinvent, and stretch any situation, idea, or feeling
that seems stuck. Improvise. How do you train to do
this? Read a lot. Go to a gallery where you like the
paintings, dioramas, sculptures, or photos. Make
little kids rap with you. Hyperbolize. Think about
what you would eat one thousand of if being full
weren't possible. Break-dance on the couch. Watch
one of the good buskers in Bloor subway for a whole
afternoon. Learn some opera. Sing it in a covered
parking lot (mad acoustics!). Consider downtown
architecture. Consider it with ninjas. Resurrect the
song you last swayed to at the end of the ninth grade
dance. Sway again. Give yourself ten nicknames.
Practice new laughs. Wear righteous socks under
suit pants. Ululate.

Why?

'Cause making fictions—in any form—has a very
real utility: it teaches you to detect all of the possible
possibilities. Maybe things ain't as bad as they feel,
given what they could be. Maybe they are, and you
need to dream in extreme ways to see alternatives. "If

the world were clear," says Al Camus, "art would not exist."

Oh, and try things that are HARD, then give yourself Pop Rocks or nap times or gin when you're done.

One year after the night at Not My Dog, my manfriend died in a freak accident.

He was a flawed madcap heart-sleeved scholar, and these kind of lightning moments of public eccentricity followed him. He laughed, clapped, and ululated. His engine ran on chaos. His death shortly after this fiery night of unexpected-life-being-lived helps me remember that exposure to the extraordinary lets us quick-reference the possibles. Always be listening for the jazz piano. Be ready to TRY THE SONG.

Now go to sleep, and dream.

Five Ways You Can Embody *Growth* Today (on Day One)

1. Ask someone the Edge of the Bed Question.
2. Buy a book of random facts (I love *Uncle John's Bathroom Reader*) and place it in your bathroom.
3. Place a box of *Trivial Pursuit* cards on your desk. Both you and others will pick them up and read them regularly. Trust me.
4. Watch a how-to video on YouTube. Doesn't matter for what.
5. Cook a new recipe.

Questions You Can Ask to Operationalize *Growth*:

- What did I do today to make it more likely someone would learn something?
- What did I do today that will make me more effective tomorrow?
- How was I a teacher today?
- How was I a student today?

TWELVE

Class

A commitment to treating people and situations better than they deserve to be treated.

QUESTION: How did I elevate instead of escalate today?

The Player to Be Named Later

Of the six values I've identified as my Day One values, class is the first one knew I wanted as part of my personal leadership culture. Well before I could define what a personal leadership culture was I knew I wanted to embody "class" in my life and it's because of one man: Crash Davis. The grizzled, thirty-something, minor-league, journeyman catcher played by Kevin Costner in the 1988 film *Bull Durham*.

I was barely a teenager when I saw the movie for the first of what is now more than fifty times. I immediately idolized Costner's character—a ballplayer spending the twilight of his career as a grudging mentor to a rookie pitcher with a "million-dollar arm and five cent head." Crash played the same position I did. He battled with umpires, debated the work of William Blake, and dispensed wisdom on life, love, and the game. At one point, Crash chastises his young protégé by tossing his fungus-covered shower shoes at him and declaring, "You'll never make it to the bigs with fungus on your shower shoes" before delivering a line that burned itself into my fourteen-year-old mind: "Think classy, you'll be classy."

From that moment on, above all else, I wanted to be classy.

Leaders Elevate

A definition of class with which I was truly happy always eluded me. The Day One approach demands a clear definition, however, and it was a former student named Hamza who delivered it as we discussed a difficult interpersonal situation with which he had recently struggled. I was impressed by his handling of the situation and told him so.

"Well," he replied, "I was just trying to elevate the situation instead of escalate it."

There was my definition: class is elevating a situation when your instincts push you to escalate, when it would be easier to escalate and when you have every right to escalate. The difference lies in your goal for the resolution of the situation: elevating means trying to succeed, escalating means trying to win. Everyone can share in success, winning necessitates someone losing. People can find common ground in the search for success, but they defend their territory in a battle to win.

In his best-selling *The 7 Habits of Highly Effective People*, Stephen Covey identified the search for win-win situations as a key practice of effective leaders and shared an important insight for leaders looking to embody class:

> *Between stimulus and response there is space. In that space is our power to choose our response. In our response lies our growth and our freedom.*

Covey didn't claim authorship of the quotation, the origin of which is a source of some debate. Regardless of where it came from, you must embrace its key lesson to equip yourself for a difficult reality: leadership isn't treating people like they deserve to be treated, it's being able to treat people *better* than they deserve to be treated. Doing so rests on your ability to respond to situations rather than react. Your happiness, success, and leadership will be determined by how you choose to use the gift of the gap between stimulus and response.

How did I elevate instead of escalate today? This question differs from my other six value-driving questions in that it's reactive: it's difficult to sit down and plan your answer in advance. The other questions drive your personal behavior—this one is triggered by the behavior of others.

Use this question as your response to confrontational situations: when you feel the urge to snap at a customer service rep, tell yourself *this moment will be the answer to How did I elevate instead of escalate today?* When you're trolled digitally or in person, tell yourself *this moment will be my answer.* When you can win the argument and leave someone hurt or let it go and move on, tell yourself *this moment will be my answer.*

The part of daily life that provides more opportunities to answer this question than anything else? Email.

Elevating Email

Our lives are driven by email. Our parents used to go to the mailbox, now we carry it with us. Entire projects are conceived, refined, and approved via email. Entire friendships take place online, and stuff that pisses us off is sent to us almost daily. You know when you get one of those emails because you talk to the screen.

Admit it—you've done it, you've seen your friends do it, you've heard your office mates do it: there's a "bing," you click, you skim a few lines, and then you hear it, "Oh, f*** off!" It's only a few seconds later you realize it was your voice.

I get emails that—let's choose a kind word here—*frustrate* me all the time. I've received emails that make my blood boil. I've received a couple that have resulted in me having to shop for a new phone. More than once in my life, I've succumbed to my base animal instincts—those leftover evolutionary urges—and fired back a response before I cooled down. Before I thought about the consequences. Hell, sometimes I thought about the consequences and did it anyway. I knew I shouldn't do it. I knew it as I was writing the email and knew it as I hit send, but I did it anyway: I escalated the situation. Oh my, did I ever. My guess is you've done it too. Some of those emails have felt great to write. Some of those emails have felt tremendous to send. Not one of those emails has ever made my life any better.

"How did I elevate instead of escalate?" has completely changed my approach to these talk-to-the-screen emails. Here's my new approach:

1. The email arrives.
2. I read it.

3. I talk to the screen. Sometimes I call in a friend. They read it and talk to the screen on my behalf.

4. I open a new document—not my email program, not Gmail, nothing with a send button. It is crucial it's a program without a send button.

5. I write the response the darkest version of me wants to write: an email that takes the other person's head off. I tell them where to go. I pour all my frustration, anger, and vitriol onto the page. Sometimes I make fun of their pets.

6. I hit "Save As" and select a folder I created a few years ago called "This Could Have Happened." I save my newly minted "up yours" manifesto into the folder and close the program.

7. I get up from my desk, walk to the other side of the room, pop in my headphones, and play one of my favorite songs. No doubt you've been told to go for a walk to cool down or to sleep on it. Both of those are tremendous ideas that often prove impractical, but you do have time in any given day to take five minutes and listen to your favorite song.

8. When the song is over, I return to my desk and open the "This Could Have Happened" folder. In it are dozens of emails that have been created by this process over the past few years. I select two at random and read them.

9. I think to myself, "Oh my God, *that* could have happened!"

10. I open my email program and write an "elevate" email. I remind myself that the foundation of any

interpersonal or organizational dysfunction is fear. People are afraid they are going to lose something: money, influence, resources, prestige. They may be afraid they're going to be given something undesirable: additional work or something for which they lack the skills, time, will, or resources. I search for the foundational fear behind the email and remind myself that any problem addressed at the level of its foundational fear rather than the behavior generated by that fear is far more likely to be solved in a productive manner. I do not counterattack. I attempt to empathize. I ask myself, "What would a great man do in response to this email?" and I endeavor to do that. I send *that* email.

Writing the first email often feels great: it's cathartic. It's good for you in some ways, but sending those emails is almost always destructive.

When your heart rate rises and adrenaline starts to flow in response to an email, comment, or perceived slight, remind yourself you've made a commitment to answer *how you elevated instead of escalated* at the end of the day. Recognize you're being given an opportunity to answer that question and live a key leadership value.

Five Ways You Can Embody *Class* Today (on Day One)

1. Apologize.
2. Think of someone at work with whom you don't get along. Swing by and offer to pick them up a coffee. Ice thaws one drip at a time.
3. Identify a moment you disagreed with someone, turned out to be wrong, and never acknowledged that fact. Go acknowledge that fact.
4. Publicly recognize a strength of someone of whom you're not particularly fond.
5. Find a way to use the phrase, "Okay, let's try it your way."

Questions You Can Ask to Operationalize *Class*:

- How did I elevate instead of escalate today?
- How did I treat someone better than they deserved to be treated today?
- What did I do today to make a difficult situation better?
- How did I admit I was wrong today?

THIRTEEN

Self-Respect

A commitment to making decisions that recognize four essential truths:

1. *You have as much right to happiness as anyone else.*
2. *You cannot add value to anyone else's life until you've added enough to your own.*
3. *Your happiness is* your *responsibility.*
4. *Happiness is not possible without forgiveness.*

Treat Yourself First

There is no hole in your life that cannot be filled by self-respect. The Day One process aims to ensure you give yourself hard evidence every day that you are someone of worth: someone who matters and deserves respect. When you believe that of yourself, you treat others as if you believe it about them.

Why should we expect our bosses, coworkers, husbands, wives, children, strangers, or the universe to do something for us we're not willing to do for ourselves: treat ourselves well? No one is going to respect you more than you respect yourself, and as such my question for embodying self-respect every day is a simple one: *What have I done today to be good to myself?*

Watch the television show you love that's beneath you intellectually (I download *Grey's Anatomy* and am entirely unapologetic about it), read the trashy magazine, listen to that cheesy pop song, or eat the cupcake. My gift to myself is a daily walk. The data on the benefits of walking for only twenty minutes is overwhelming, but I dedicate a couple of hours each day. Adding audiobooks or presentation rehearsal to a portion of my walks turned them from something for which I was "too busy" to a restorative and productive part of my day that I almost never miss.

Being good to yourself can take on a lot of different forms, some of which you may not have considered before. This chapter will provide six practices that make being good to yourself each day a little bit easier:

1. Recognize that happiness must be cultivated.
2. Recognize that greatest is the enemy of great.
3. Stop wearing your fake leg.
4. Plan for failure.
5. Recognize that things don't happen for a reason.
6. Heal.

Recognize That Happiness Must Be Cultivated

Believing your happiness must be generated by someone else will doom you to a life that lacks it. That's not to say you shouldn't surround yourself with people who love you, empower you, and support you at your lowest points—I hope the people with whom you interact treat you with respect, generosity, kindness, and compassion. You deserve that from others, but you're not *entitled* to it. Believing you're entitled to happiness from external sources makes it less likely you'll develop the capacity required to generate it for yourself.

What have I done today to be good to myself is intended to build that capacity: to increase the percentage of your happiness generated *internally* and make you less dependent on the behavior of others for your happiness and satisfaction. It allows you to adopt an important perspective: on days when no one delivers you happiness, you haven't been slighted—you've been denied a privilege. While you can hope that privilege returns, you are capable of surviving without it. Externally delivered happiness is the emotional equivalent of your cell phone: you don't feel you can live without it but certainly have the capacity to do so.

We're capable of generating our own happiness on most days: by hitting the gym, having coffee with a friend, dancing in our living room, or eating that cupcake. However, there are some days when we are so stressed, so hurt, so exhausted, or have been hit by pain so significant we simply don't have it in us to try to bring something good into our lives. It's for those days that we must *cultivate* happiness.

Deep in one of my depressive episodes, a dear friend taught me the concept of *cultivating happiness*. She explained we must plant seeds for anything we wish to harvest in the future and happiness is no exception.

"On your good days," she told me, "you must plant a seed for your future happiness. Do something good for that stressed, hurt, frustrated, or exhausted version of yourself in the future. Something specific—something your future self will thank you for." I put this approach into action shortly after.

There's little predictability in my life: I travel up to 250 days a year so I'm often in a different place with a different schedule and demands each day. One consistency: you'll usually find me standing in front of a PowerPoint presentation. For years my presentations were stark and boring: a white font against a black background to accommodate any kind of venue lighting.

A few weeks after the seed for cultivating happiness was planted for me, I was having a great day on the road. Travel had been seamless, the hotel was beautiful, my hosts could not have been more kind, and the audience had been wonderfully receptive. Upon returning to my hotel room, my phone beeped with an appointment reminder. I've scheduled reminders that pop up with all my Day One questions, four times a day. It's my catalyst for keeping them front and center in my priorities. *What have I done today to be good to myself?* caught my eye.

That morning I'd added a photograph of me with a koala bear from a recent speaking tour of Australia. It had gotten a big laugh and I had smiled thinking about the tremendous day I spent with a dear friend when it was taken. I popped it onto my screen again to remind myself how lucky I was to have that person in my life. Staring at the photo, I heard my friend's words pop into my head: "You have to cultivate happiness."

My days on the road aren't always as good as that one: some days travel is not so seamless, the hotel room's thermostat is set permanently to 85 degrees, and the audience is too hung over to care what I have to say. That day in my hotel room I chose to do something good for the version of me who would be experiencing that day in the future. Searching photographs from my past few years of travel, I began placing my favorites in the background of my slides. Each of those photographs represents a moment of peace, joy, wonder, and gratitude. My presentations now deliver dozens of reminders of how incredibly lucky I've been in my life. I planted those moments years ago and they have been generating happiness almost every day since.

What's something you could do today that would cultivate a moment of happiness for you each day in the future? If you drive to work without the photograph of someone you love hanging from the mirror you're missing an opportunity to make yourself smile each day. If you don't drive, place the photo on the back of the front door of your house. Pick five friends, assign them days of the week, and ask them to send you something they think will make you laugh on their assigned day. Return the favor for them. You'll find that whatever you send will be something that makes you smile as well.

Your happiness is in your job description—plan for it today and cultivate it for the future.

Recognize That Greatest Is the Enemy of Great

I'm going to return one last time to that transformative train trip across the country to share one final lesson that it taught me—fittingly, during my last meal of the trip.

The trip's two biggest personalities boarded in Montreal for the trip's final leg. They were two hard-drinking, larger-than-life former east coasters with booming laughs, seemingly endless stories, and an apparently inexhaustible supply of energy.

They were both more than eighty years old.

Ten minutes out of Montreal they burst into the bar car, drinks in hand, and proceeded to vigorously shake hands with everyone they found there.

"I'm Jimmy, this is Earl," Jimmy would tell you, grinning.

Earl would take your hand immediately afterward. "I'm Earl, that was Jimmy."

They made a beeline for the bar, bought a round for everyone there, and made a point of clinking glasses with every last one of us. Taking seats at a table in the middle of the lounge, they proceeded to hold court. Jokes and stories began to flow. The two of them had been friends for over sixty years and for forty-five of those years had taken the train from Montreal to Halifax to visit family for a week. A small crowd gathered to listen, and as others heard the constant bursts of laughter, the crowd grew increasingly larger.

"Hey, has anyone got a guitar?" Jimmy shouted at one point. Someone ran back to his room and returned with a guitar. For the next hour Jimmy and Earl harmonized through a variety of east coast tunes, and by the end we had all joined in with them.

It was after midnight when things finally broke up and I hung around to ask the two of them if they might be willing to let me join them for lunch the next day. The train would arrive in Halifax late afternoon, so lunch would be the final meal served on the train. I knew there could not be a better duo with which to spend it.

"We'd be happy to!" bellowed Earl. "You just have to bring us something!"

Judging from what I'd seen that evening I assumed a bottle of single malt, but he surprised me with his request.

"I want you to bring me a list of the five things you'd do tomorrow if you knew you were going to die at the end of the day," he said.

"God, what for?" I asked. It seemed like a bit of a macabre exercise.

"Because at our ages, that might very well happen," Jimmy replied with a wink. "So, we like seeing if anyone's got any good ideas!"

I made the deal and found myself sitting across from Jimmy and Earl the next day at lunch. They slipped easily into the banter friends who have known each other forever use to amuse others—it's almost like a performance. As the waitress dropped off our food, Jimmy turned his attention to me and asked, "So Drew, what exactly is it that you do?"

"I run a university leadership development program," I replied.

"Ah, so you work with students?" asked Jimmy.

"Yes sir," I told him.

"Well then, what is the one thing you want your students to walk away having learned?"

"I want them to recognize that they are leaders already but that they can be better ones if they create a plan to do so every day," I told him. "The problem is a lot of my students are focused on the wrong things."

"Oh really?" said Earl, raising his eyebrow. "What do you mean?"

"Well," I said, "let me give you an example. The first time I get a group of students together, I ask, 'How many of you know what your GPA was last semester?' Every hand in the room goes up. Then I ask them, 'How many of you know how much money you made per hour at your last job?' Every hand in the room goes up. I ask them, 'How many of you know who sings "Party in the USA"?' Every hand goes up."

"Miley Cyrus," Earl offered helpfully.

"He's a fan," Jimmy said in response to my shocked look.

I laughed. "Well, yes. But marks, money, Miley Cyrus… they know them all. Then I ask them, 'How many of you can tell me the single happiest moment of your life?' And hardly any hands go up."

I sat back. I had told that story a lot and had gotten used to people shaking their heads in disappointment at my students—a tacit confirmation that I was in the right for showing them the problem with their priorities. Earl looked at me for a moment before offering his take.

"That's because that's a dumb-ass question."

This was not the reaction I was used to.

"What? 'What's the happiest moment in your life?' is a dumb-ass question?" I asked incredulously. "You don't think it's important for someone to be self-aware enough to identify the happiest moment in their life? To prioritize knowing that ahead of how much money they make or what their grades are?"

Earl shook his head. "If you're someone who's teaching people, I think it's more important that you're aware of how dangerous that question is."

"Dangerous? What do you mean?" I asked.

"Look," said Earl. "The problem with asking people to think about the happiest moment of their life, or the most beautiful sunset, or the most delicious meal, or the best kiss, or the greatest sex, is that there's only *one* of those things in anyone's life. There can be only one happiest, greatest, most beautiful of anything. That's what those words mean—the single best one."

He leaned forward.

"But Drew, there are so many great moments in our lives. So many sunsets, so many meals, and," he grinned mischievously, "if you're lucky an awful lot of kisses and sex. The problem with your question is it reinforces the idea that only the things at the very top deserve celebration. I think that means moments and meals and sunsets that are actually amazing get diminished in our minds just because they're not the greatest we've ever had. I think it's dangerous to teach people something that might make them diminish good things in their lives."

I was stunned at how much sense his logic made. "I never

even considered that," I told him. "But what do you suggest I do instead?"

"Tell them to draw a line," Earl replied, dragging his finger horizontally across the table in front of us. "A line in their mind that represents great. For everything they experience in life their only question should be, 'Did that fall above the great line'? If it did, file it there. There's unlimited room above the great line. Your goal in life should be to create as big a collection of things above the great line as you can in as many different categories as you can: a big pile of great conversations, meals, successes, perspectives, and yeah, some more of the sex too."

"Think of it like poker," Jimmy jumped in. "Your goal is to have the biggest stack of chips. That's the same thing with life. If you only focus on the greatest of everything in your life, you'll get one chip for each category: sunsets, laughs, whatever. But if you focus on collecting things above the great line, you can create this monstrous stack in every category. That's a lot more chips than someone who just looks at the greatest of everything."

"Basically, Drew," Earl jumped back in, " 'greatest' is the enemy of 'great.' "

Greatest is the enemy of great is wisdom that I've passed along at every opportunity since that moment, but right then I wanted to know where it had come from.

"How did you come up with that approach to life?" I asked Earl.

He shrugged. "I guess it's probably because when I was sixteen I had what I figured was going to be the single greatest moment in my life, and the thought of living my life knowing

I was never going to top it kinda sucked…so I cooked up a different approach."

"You had the single greatest moment of your life at sixteen?" I asked him.

"What I thought was going to be," he responded. "The day I met him." He gestured to Jimmy. "On Juno Beach."

"Wait," I said. "Juno Beach? As in D-Day?"

The two of them nodded.

"Yep," said Jimmy. "I was halfway up the beach, facedown in the sand, and I look up, and this idiot is standing there, maybe twenty feet in front of me, yanking like crazy at some defensive fence post that had been set up. Just standing there. I figured he was going to get his head blown off, so I started screaming at him to get down. Of course, you couldn't hear anything, but for some reason I became obsessed with getting this idiot to duck!"

Earl put his hands up in the classic "whatcha gonna do?" pose.

Jimmy continued. "I just kept screaming and screaming, but he couldn't hear me. Finally, I don't know what the hell came over me, but I got so damn frustrated I stood up to scream at him. Bullets and bombs everywhere and I stand up to yell at this jackass."

"I heard him though!" Earl chirped up.

"Yeah, he did," said Jimmy, with a look of fake anger I knew had been honed over thousands of tellings of this story over the years. "He turned around to look at me. Big stupid look on his face."

"Hey," said Earl, "I was doing just fine until you yelled at me. As soon as I turned around, though, caught myself a German bullet right off the side of my arm."

"Yeah," said Jimmy through clenched teeth, "and the son of a bitch redirected it right off mine!"

With that the two of them rolled up their sleeves to reveal matching scars.

"Same damn bullet got us both," Earl said with a grin. "We've been friends ever since."

"That's unreal!" I exclaimed.

Earl shook his head. "It was all unreal, Drew. I've never been as scared before or since. As soon as I hit the beach, I just knew I was going to die. There was no question in my mind. I made a lot of deals with the Big Guy that day I'll tell ya."

He got quiet for a moment before continuing. "After we both got hit, we just went looking for cover. We got ourselves dug in and I don't really remember what happened next. But when I remember coming back to my senses it was quiet, and I remember realizing that I was still alive, and it was the most remarkable, indescribable feeling of happiness. There were two things I knew at that moment. One was 'I'll never feel this happy again in my life,' and the second was, 'I'll never end another day with anything left on my list.'"

I was mesmerized by his story but didn't get this reference.

"What do you mean by your list?" I asked.

"Ah," said Earl. "Did you bring what I asked you to bring?"

I had in fact spent the night before pondering what I would do if I knew I was going to die at the end of the next day. It had been a tough exercise and I encourage you to take a moment to do the same thing as soon as you can.

"I did!" I said, reaching for my pocket. Earl held up his hand.

"No, you don't have to tell me what they are," he said. "I just want you to look at it. Look at those five things and ask yourself if there's a single one of them you're incapable of doing."

I glanced at the list. Everything on it was certainly within my power and ability to pull off.

"There isn't," I told Earl.

"Are there any you actually plan on doing today?" he asked.

I looked at the list again. For a long moment.

"No," I said quietly.

Earl nodded. "You see, my friend, that's where we're different. I never go to bed with anything left on that list."

He leaned back in his chair. "By the way," he said, "you should know this: I was totally wrong. I did feel that happy again in my life. More than once actually. I'm lucky I was convinced I wouldn't so early on. It made me appreciate a lot more in this life. Experiencing what it feels like to know there's no tomorrow has really changed the way I deal with today."

What have I done today to be good to myself? I've used what I learned over that lunch to be good to myself many times in the years since. While I can't claim that I never use terms like "greatest," "best," or "most amazing/beautiful" to describe experiences in my life, I usually catch myself and am reminded simply to file those memories away above the great line in my mind.

"That goes above the great line" is a thought that goes through my head a lot. I've said it pushing back from a great meal, watching the sun set out the window of a plane, or hiking through an extraordinary neighborhood in one of the world's great cities. I believe that any day you put something above the great line, your recognition of that fact can serve as your answer to "What have I done today to be good to myself?"

The fact that we have the rest of our lives ahead of us is the biggest reason we don't do things today that will make the rest of our lives better. Three of the five items on my list that day started with the word "forgive": there were three relationships I hoped to make a part of my life again but had continually come up with a reason to put off making it happen. Within a week of meeting Jimmy and Earl, two of them were once again a part of my life and in the years since have made it significantly better. I try to emulate Earl's philosophy of never going to bed with something left on the list. Doing so puts off something that will make my life better today.

Stop Wearing Your Fake Leg

My friend Stephanie Dixon is a force of nature.

Stephanie has represented Canada at the Athens, Sydney, and Beijing Paralympic Games. She is a member of the Canadian Sports Hall of Fame and the Order of Canada (perhaps Canada's highest honor). She has seventeen medals, five world records, and one leg. She's one of the greatest Paralympians in Canadian history and is even more impressive as a human being.

Being around someone capable of the discipline and

sacrifice necessary to become a world-class performer is intimidating, and I found myself dwelling on insecurities about my life and career while having dinner with her one night. I was sharing negative feedback I had been getting over the previous few months: people felt I wasn't growing my company fast enough; that I was traveling too much and not making my book a priority; that I was placing too much of a focus on keeping my life balanced and was missing opportunities as a result. I was worried they might be right: Was I being aggressive enough? Ambitious enough? Was I working hard enough?

"Drew," Stephanie said suddenly, cutting me off, "are you happy with your career?"

"I'm thrilled with my career," I answered. "It's better than I ever could have imagined!"

"Are you happy with your life?" she asked.

"Very much so," I replied.

"Well then, Drew," she said, staring hard at me, "you need to stop wearing your fake leg."

"Um...sorry?" was all that I could manage.

"Look," she said, "I was born without a right hip, so prosthetics don't do an awful lot for me. I'm much faster on just a pair of crutches and one leg. But for years I wore a fake leg all the time, especially to school, because when I didn't it made the other kids uncomfortable. That fake leg slowed me down and hurt like hell, but I wore it to make others happier with who I was—so that I didn't make other people uncomfortable."

She gestured in my direction. "Almost everybody has got a fake leg in their life. Anything that you keep in your life that slows you down and hurts you, and the only reason that it's still in your life is it makes who you are and what you're doing more palatable to other people—that's your fake leg. You worrying about whether your company is big enough for other people, or whether you've written the book that they would have written, or whatever? That's you're fake leg."

She leaned in. "Drew, when you wear your fake leg what you're saying to other people is that 'your normal deserves more respect than my normal.' Well guess what? If you don't respect your normal, who the hell else will?"

What are you keeping in your life that's slowing you down and hurting you? What's your fake leg and why are you still wearing it? Be willing to examine your life each day and identify the parts you're keeping only to please others. Removing those parts is an essential part of a personal culture of leadership.

Plan for Failure

In early April 2013, a TEDx Talk I had delivered a few weeks earlier in Washington, DC, was posted online. I clicked on the link sent by the event organizer and watched as my image appeared on the screen. I was horrified by what I saw: I simply did not realize I had gotten so huge. That may seem ridiculous given I was looking into a mirror every day, but there's something different about seeing yourself in a photograph or on-screen. I had always battled with my weight and I suppose I knew that it had gotten out of control, but somehow I'd managed to deny it. This was even as my weight crept over 300 pounds, airline seat belts became a source of stress and embarrassment, and once, in a humiliating moment, I was told by the operator of a ride at Universal Studios that "the ride cannot safely accommodate your dimensions, sir."

As I looked at myself on-screen that day I couldn't deny it any longer: something had to be done. I could no longer stand in front of audiences and talk about a value like self-respect when I was consistently making choices that were bad for my health. How could I talk about courage when I clearly didn't have enough to take on the challenge of becoming a healthier person? My messages about commitment and disciplined daily execution were being undermined by my obviously out-of-control eating.

I needed to do something. I even knew I could do it because ten years earlier I had managed to lose sixty pounds in a matter of a few months. Unfortunately, the fact I had done it before was a roadblock to me doing it again. I can't count how many times I sat in my apartment having just consumed one and a half large pizzas (my standard order was two, so there would be half left for breakfast), or three twelve-inch subs, or an entire bucket of KFC on my own, feeling absolutely disgusted with myself but saying: "Don't worry too much about it—you know that if you just decide to dedicate yourself you can dump all this weight, just like you did before. It'll take a few months, but you can do it, and you *will* do it soon. This is one of the last times you'll binge like this." The knowledge I had done it before meant I didn't feel I had to prove it to myself again. It was just a matter of deciding when to start, and I was okay with putting that off for a little while. Looking at that video, I wasn't okay with it any longer.

I just wasn't sure where to begin. I had tried the same tactics I used the decade before on more than one occasion, but I wasn't twenty-three anymore, my metabolism was different, and it simply wasn't working.

Then it hit me: I knew where to begin—on Day One. I needed to take the same approach to weight loss I used to operationalize my leadership values every day. I needed a set of questions that would drive the actions necessary to start my weight-loss journey *today*. If I took the first steps toward health on Day One, all I had to do was repeat Day One again and again. If I did that, I'd eventually hit my weight-loss goal.

While I had experience creating questions to operationalize values, I had no idea what questions would lead to the behaviors needed to lose weight. I've learned three of the most important words in leadership are "I don't know," so I took that question to a close friend of mine. I'm sure you have a friend just like her: they have multiple sets of running shoes (to deal with different weather conditions), they run a 10K on Sunday morning before you've gotten out of bed, they can name more than one kind of yoga, and they spend what you feel is a disconcerting amount of time talking about whatever the hell "macros" are. She was a certified nutritionist and fitness freak, so I asked her simply: *What questions do I need to ask and answer each day to be 100 pounds lighter one year from today?*

She took note of my age, height, and weight and told me she'd get back to me. She invited me for coffee two days later and delivered two insights that changed my life. The first was my three Day One weight-loss questions:

1. Have I eaten less than 1,800 calories today?
2. Have I burned more than 3,000 calories today?
3. Have I done fifteen more seconds of cardio than yesterday?

The second was far more important.

"Drew," she said. "Failure is a part of life, it's inevitable. You should build failure into absolutely every plan you create. Don't create a contingency plan *in case* you fail, build the inevitable failure into your plan at the outset. Anything that isn't part of your plan kills momentum, so if failure is already built in, it sucks, but it's not a momentum killer.

"So," she continued. "We're building in sixty-five days of failure. You get sixty-five days—more than two months—where you don't have to answer those questions. Use them if you're too stressed, or too tired, or you're speaking at a banquet and don't want to be rude. You get sixty-five days and the only restriction is you don't get to use any of them in the first two weeks."

That was it: three questions I had to answer on Day One and then I had to live Day One over and over again for 300 of the next 365 days. I was 100.7 pounds lighter one year to the day after she gave me those questions.

I treated every one of those days like Day One. It was hardest in the evenings, when powerful cravings would start a battle with myself over whether to use one of my sixty-five days. Whenever the battle began I told myself the same thing: "You can go over 1,800 calories on day two. Tomorrow is day two," and I meant it every single time. When I woke up the next morning though, the absolute first thing I thought to myself was: "Yesterday was a win. I answered the questions. That day goes on a pile and when that pile hits 300, I'll be 100 pounds lighter than when I started. Nothing can take yesterday off that pile." Every morning I said that felt like a victory. It gave me the momentum and confidence I needed to immediately say: "Today is Day One again."

I could eat over 1,800 calories on day two, but the first sixty-seven days of my weight-loss journey were Day One. There were a few day twos along the way, but I aimed to live each day like Day One—knowing a pile of 300 Day Ones represented a once-unattainable goal.

Day One leadership doesn't have a specific number of wins that will take you to where you want to be, but it will drive behavior that brings consistent benefits. You must build in failure, however: recognize you won't be able to answer all your questions each day. Aim to get two-thirds of your questions answered 300 out of 365 days of the year.

Remember that failures are reps for your resilience muscle. Reminding yourself that failure is not a threat to your plan but rather an expected part of it is a great way to answer *What did I do today to be good to myself?*

The Five Steps of Everything

I give myself permission to view failure as inevitable by remembering that there are five steps to anything you try to accomplish:

1. **The First Step**—"I love to write, but I hate to start," wrote my favorite writer. If we don't take the first step, we avoid inevitable missteps, but standing

still can be the biggest misstep of all. Look at your bank account: if you'd put $100 a month away starting when you were eighteen, you would be able to afford that down payment right now. If you'd started running an extra half mile per week a year ago you could finish a marathon tomorrow. Your life doesn't change until you take the first step in a new direction.

2. **The Next Step**—The first step may be hard but it's the next step that's truly scary. It's easy to turn back after the first step (ask anyone who has started a diet) but the next step truly commits you. If crafting your business idea is the first step, the moment you hand in your resignation is the next step. After the next step there's no turning back—you're something different than you were before.

3. **The Wrong Step**—After deciding to get somewhere you will at some point try to go about doing so in a fashion that simply does not work. The wrong step may only take you a short distance from the right path, or you may end up straying much farther. Odds are you will not build your business, personal relationships, or your road through life perfectly in one try. Denying you've taken the wrong step means you won't move on to step 4.

4. **The Step Back**—Somewhere along the line, we equated change with failure and began to believe changing our business plan, timelines, or personal

or professional partners meant admitting to ourselves and everyone watching we made a mistake with our initial decision. Business is an exploration. *Life* is an exploration—and true exploration isn't possible without a willingness to acknowledge mistakes and embrace change. When you equate change with failure you create a roadblock to the acceptance of a crucial truth: the only way to avoid large mistakes is to acknowledge the small ones and be willing to back up to a spot before your misstep.

5. **The New Step**—This is the most courageous of the steps. The moment we take a step back to ask "Which way do I go now?" we're often at our most insecure. Our wrong step is still fresh in our minds and it takes courage to step in a new direction when we know it could happen again. It's in this step that most of our dreams live or die. We can see ourselves standing at the edge of a cliff in this moment. Reframe that imagery: think not about facing the cliff edge, but facing away, showing it your back. Only with a stride forward will you move toward safety. The real danger lies in backing up too far.

Every aspect of your life will feature iterations of this cycle: your professional life, your relationships, health, and education. You will likely have several of these cycles going at once. Don't try to minimize or shut them down—they're a natural part of dynamic lives. Each step brings its own set of fears—a set of fears everyone faces. Hiding our fears denies us the mutual support that comes from telling one another, "You're not the only one." These steps are inevitable: embracing your journeys through them is key to success and happiness in business and life. After all, continuing to put one foot in front of the other will always take you somewhere.

Recognize That Things Don't Happen for a Reason

A friend of mine had been on the fast track at a major marketing firm before severe health issues forced her to take a leave of absence and eventually leave her job entirely. As she had battled to regain her health, her mother had passed away. What followed were several years of some of the most remarkable strength, patience, and perseverance I've seen from a human being. As she slowly recovered both physically and emotionally, she discovered a new passion. At first it was a hobby, then a small business, then a larger one. We were meeting to toast a major milestone in her business, and she was beaming as she sat across from me.

"I've never been happier," she told me. "My life is better than I ever thought possible."

"You've earned it," I told her. "You fought your way through a lot."

"Everything happens for a reason!" she told me.

I physically cringed. *Everything happens for a reason* is a cultural cliché I can't stand.

I like the sentiment: given enough time even things that

seem to hurt us can provide opportunities for growth, even rewards. However, we can't forget that the time between our pain and that payoff is characterized by our strength, patience, and perseverance.

Strength, patience, and perseverance: those are the reasons positive things can grow out of the negative things that happen to us. When our strength, patience, and perseverance take us through the dark times in our lives and eventually provide us with an opportunity for growth and happiness, we shouldn't flippantly attribute that opportunity to some "grand plan" over which we have no control. Doing so fails to recognize our strength and give ourselves the credit we both deserve and need. If we don't treat our previous successes as evidence we're capable of future success, we fail to plant seeds of confidence that will later grow into the roots of optimism.

There is no reason for anything, there are *reasons* for everything. Optimism and strength are born from letting go of the idea that we are more likely to fail than we are to succeed. Look at the evidence: your success rate on surviving and moving forward is 100 percent. Every piece of evidence in your past points to the fact that you will have a future. If you're still here reading this, you can't identify a single challenge in your life that you didn't survive.

Optimism comes from recognizing that having almost broken before does not make it more likely you will break next time. You are not plastic or glass—where each crack or bend brings the inevitable collapse closer—you are muscle, where being torn down means growing back stronger.

Sometimes the things that bring you closest to breaking are in fact the things that one day will keep you from breaking. You have dealt with every single problem you have ever faced because you are still here. You may not be pleased with how you dealt with problems and you may have acquired some scars along the way, but you've dealt with them all. Acknowledge the support, love, friendship, and greater powers that helped, but never diminish the role of your own strength and perseverance.

Everything happens for a reason? Yes, and *you're* the reason. You've been the reason every time and the strength that has gotten you this far has not diminished, even if it sometimes feels otherwise. Never forget the battles you have fought and won: they are evidence of your past successes, and a case for what you can accomplish in the future.

Heal

Healing isn't often associated with leadership because it's tied to the idea of hurt in the same way leadership is deeply intertwined with the idea of strength. We see leaders as strong, and believe strong people don't get hurt. There's a bit of an unspoken understanding that if you're type of person who gets hurt a lot, leadership probably isn't for you.

The most extraordinary leaders I've known are the ones who are the best at healing. They recognize it is a skill that must be practiced and make it a part of their daily lives. They accept that attempting to live a life of impact, courage, empowerment, growth, class, and self-respect means you're going to make yourself vulnerable at times and that hurt—both intentional and inadvertent—is inevitable. As such, leaders must have faith in their ability to heal.

Each one of my six value-driving questions carries with it the possibility of being hurt:

- You could attempt to recognize someone else's leadership only to have them tell you they couldn't care less what you think of them.
- You could try something that might not work, and have it not work in a way that's both embarrassing and very public.
- You could try to support someone in the pursuit of a goal only to end up knocking them two steps backward.
- You could endeavor to learn something new only to discover that despite your best efforts, you simply cannot master it.
- You could try to elevate a situation only to find that the person willing to sling mud finds their efforts rewarded and profits at your expense.
- You could attempt to "take off your fake leg" and demand others respect your normal only to find that they refuse and neither respect nor support you moving forward.

No one likes to be hurt, but if you have faith in your ability to heal, it makes finding that five seconds of extraordinary courage a little bit easier. Without faith in your ability to heal, doing something that could result in hurt makes little sense to your brain. Its job is to keep you safe—to steer you away from damage from which you might not recover. Show your mind that you can recover, and it becomes more daring.

I believe strongly in my ability to heal. I don't appreciate being hurt but I don't fear it the way I used to. Getting to this point hasn't been an easy journey and I was helped along by remarkable insights from others, including another powerful one from the man whose story I used to open the book: Mustafa.

Think Like a Landlord

Mustafa's insight that we should "live every day like it's our first day" clearly left an impression on me—I've shared it in hundreds of presentations around the world, and its spirit is obviously embodied in the entire concept of Day One. It had a much different effect on me the first time I heard him say it. For a minute or so I found it wildly inspiring, but it wasn't long before my mood started to change.

I was on that Middle Eastern tour only six weeks after leaving my job at the university. I had loved my job for most of my time there: I loved the students, building the leadership program, the plans we had for the future, and the momentum we had built. What I didn't love is someone I had to work with: we had fundamental differences in perspectives and values, and though we both attempted to find a way to work through them, our relationship continued to deteriorate. Eventually I was getting physically ill before going to work each day and felt I had no choice but to leave the university.

The thing was I didn't feel like I had chosen to leave, I felt that I had been pushed out. Ultimately it was my decision, but I believed there had been a conscious effort to create an environment so toxic that leaving would be the only rational choice.

Listening to Mustafa talk about how much he loved his job—how he still felt the same energy and passion on day 5,000 as he had on Day One—I began thinking about the job I had left behind, about the things we had started building I'd never see come to fruition. I began to dwell on how I felt I had been mistreated, how unfair the situation had been, and, of course, I started thinking about the person I held responsible for all of it.

When you think about a conflict your body starts to react like it is still in the conflict, and I grew quiet and tense as I sat next to Mustafa. He grew concerned at this sudden change in my demeanor.

"Mr. Dudley," he said, "I'm so sorry. Did I say something to offend you?"

"Oh no, Mustafa," I said quickly, not wanting him to blame himself for my sudden somber mood. "It's just..." The entire story came rushing out. I told a (basically) complete stranger a deeply personal story about one of the most intense conflicts in my life.

When I finally finished, Mustafa drove in silence for what must have been a full minute before saying quietly, "Mr. Dudley, this person that you speak about—they are so far away! They are so far away that it is night where they are and it is day where you are. Yet you are letting them make it night where you are."

He made a sweeping gesture at the extraordinary desert that surrounded us. "You are letting them wreck Mustafa's

Grand Adventure and they are not even here! What's worse, you're acting like it is somehow their fault!"

Now, when you tell someone else the story of an interpersonal conflict, one of the benefits of being the storyteller is you get to recount the story in such a way as to make it very clear that it's the other person's fault, so I was a little taken aback by his reaction.

"But it is their fault!" I protested.

Mustafa shook his head. "With respect, Mr. Dudley, this is your fault." He said. "It is your fault because you are not thinking like a landlord."

"I don't understand," I said.

"My father told me to always think like a landlord," explained Mustafa. "A landlord allows people to use his property, but he charges rent to protect his investment. Your head and your heart are the most valuable pieces of property that you will ever control. If you are going to allow people access to your head and your heart, you have got to get something valuable in return. This person you're talking about—all they bring you is anger and bitterness and sadness. Anger and bitterness and sadness are not valuable to anyone. But when you accept anger and bitterness and sadness in return for access to your head and your heart, you are basically letting someone else live there rent free."

He glanced over at me for a moment. "Drew, the landlord sets the rent. You are the landlord. You're not allowed to be angry when all you get paid is what you asked for."

Spending a day with Mustafa was like going dune bashing with Yoda. I've heard the phrase "don't let people live rent free in your head" in a variety of places in the years since, but it was Mustafa who first explained the concept to me.

Not everything to which we are connected brings us value. Being a leader means finding a way to identify the things in our lives from which we must disconnect: the things we are allowing to live rent free in our heads.

I was once the producer of a musical project—a compilation CD dedicated to the memory of a friend lost to cancer. A set of lyrics from one of the songs has stayed with me:

> There's a difference between grounded and run into the ground.
> Some things keep you rooted, and some just weigh you down
> and you have to decide what you'd rather keep around.
> —"Safe and Sound" by Joyce Saunders

Healing comes from having the ability to look at the connections in your life and ask honestly: "Which of these things are keeping me rooted, and which of these things are weighing me down?" The things weighing you down are the things living rent free in your head. They can be relationships, failures, losses, and sometimes most damaging, the perception of who it is that we're *supposed* to be.

"The Man You're Going to Be One Day"

My parents let me throw the "End of High School Party": the one that closes every teen coming-of-age movie. I hosted it at our family cottage and it was filled with all the beer- and angst-fueled mayhem you'd expect from high school's last hurrah.

Halfway through the party two of my friends who were dating snuggled up to watch the sun go down about twenty feet from me. My teenage insecurity was fueled by a couple of pints and I turned to my buddy Scott and said, "Scott, it sucks that I don't have somebody like that. I'm so tired of always being alone."

Scotty was that friend who seemed to have it all: an all-star athlete and kick-ass musician who had good looks and a tremendous sense of humor. In other words, everything I thought I wasn't. He looked at me and said: "Drew, for a guy who's got everything going for him, all I ever hear from you is about what you don't have."

I was not yet at the point in my life when I wanted my friends to tell me what I needed to hear as opposed to what I wanted to hear, so I pushed back: "I don't have everything going for me. All I have is pressure. All I have is people telling me to make sure you keep getting those amazing marks. Make sure you live up to your potential. I feel like all I have is an opportunity to disappoint everyone. To be a failure in front of everybody who believes in me."

Scott looked at me for what seemed like a long time. Finally, he said, "Drew, you've got to give your friends more credit. We don't care about you because of the guy you might be one day. We care about you because of the guy you are now. I think you have to start to do the same thing."

His words have stuck with me for my entire life: never diminish the person you are by comparing yourself to the person you might be one day.

Unfortunately, only a few weeks later Scott and another

friend were killed in a car accident just outside of my hometown. He was eighteen years old. More than twenty years later I share his insight all over the world. The fact that he was a teenager does not diminish his leadership. I share his insights because he mattered, and so do you.

Shortly after Scott's death I headed to university, snagging a job bartending at the campus pub. One of the senior staff members, a guy named Jason Abraham, had a quiet charisma I couldn't help but admire: people were drawn to him and he had become one of the most popular people on campus.

One night after work, I asked Jason, "How do you connect so easily with people? How is it so many of the people here are drawn to you?"

He flushed a little and said, "You know what? I just try to keep it simple. I think that your life is better if you avoid situations where you're forced to say, 'I'm sorry.' The easiest way to avoid 'I'm sorry's' is this: every time you talk about somebody, act as if they're standing directly behind you. Your life just gets easier."

That's how Jason talked and that's how Jason lived. Unfortunately, just a few weeks after he gave me that advice he was diagnosed with cancer. Within five weeks, he was gone.

Jason Abraham was twenty-three years old, and I share what he taught me with the leaders of Fortune 500 companies because he mattered and because he was a leader. So are you.

I'm forty-one years old and I've been to nine friends' weddings and eighteen friends' funerals. I could write a full chapter on how each of the friends I buried made me a better leader, and fifteen of them didn't live to see their twenty-fourth birthday. But they mattered, and they were leaders. So are you.

I share the stories of my friends not to make people sad, but because sharing their stories continues to help me heal from their loss. I share them to remind others that your ability to matter, to impact, to share with others pieces of your story that make their lives better—in short, to lead—is in no way correlated to your age, level of education, how much money you have, what your title is, or how smart you think you are. It *is* correlated to your willingness to act in a way that makes it more likely you will have a positive impact on your own life and on the lives of others each and every day.

Only Hurt People Hurt Others

I often highlight the insights of friends I've lost when I speak to young people, aiming to reinforce that leadership begins at any age. A young woman approached me a few years ago and said, "Drew, I really liked your presentation, but I feel bad for all the pain you have had in your life." Then she told me *her* story: a story with far more courage, many more challenges, and loss more profound than I had experienced at that time. When she had finished, I looked at her and said, "How can you tell me you feel bad for the pain I've had in my life when yours so obviously dwarfs mine?"

"I've discovered that there's no universal measuring unit for pain. Hurt just hurts," she replied. "Anything less than what you've grown accustomed to is pain, so comparing it is pointless. I've learned to never judge my pain against others', and never to judge the pain of others against my own."

Her next statement floored me: "Only hurt people hurt others," she said. "So, if I want to be the woman I know I can be, I've got to let go of the things that hurt me."

Only hurt people hurt others is an essential insight for leadership and life. It means leaders have got to forgive and leaders have got to heal. If we don't evict the things living rent free in our heads, we will carry them with us and one day use them as weapons against those we care about most.

Leaders must forgive but the problem is we want to *win*. We know the things living rent free are sucking value from our lives but we're not willing to evict them until we feel we've won. We don't want an ex-partner, ex-friend, or ex-boss out there thinking that they inflicted the most hurt or got one over on us. We know we should let these conflicts go and are totally willing to do so—as soon as someone acknowledges that "we were in the right."

After losing so many friends in ways I cannot control, I am driven to share this advice: if you can save a relationship—family, romantic, friendship, professional—by simply saying "I'm sorry" or hearing "I'm sorry," do so. There is no worse feeling than going to a funeral of someone you cared about when the last thing you said to them was terrible. It has happened to me twice. True leadership means going to bed every night knowing it's not a possibility.

I'm betting you have someone you wish was still in your life: someone you could call, text, or have coffee with to share triumphs and losses. I'd lay odds the only reason you can't is because you're not willing to say, "I'm sorry" or hear "I'm sorry" (and the latter is often more difficult than the former).

You want to know the absolute best way to answer the question *What have I done today to be good to myself?* Reach out to that person. The single act that would most dramatically improve your life at this moment is forgiveness. There is no weakness in forgiveness and leadership begins where forgiveness begins.

That does not mean forgiveness is easy. You can't snap your fingers and forgive everyone who has ever hurt you or made you feel like less than you are. I haven't done it successfully—I'm still carrying things with me. What you do is—you guessed it—ask a powerful question every day: *"What is living rent free in my head, and am I ready to let it go?"* Forgive yourself when the answer isn't yes today. It might not be yes tomorrow or for a long time after that, but any question asked every day is going to be answered sooner than one that isn't. Leadership isn't about knowing all the answers. Leadership is being willing to keep asking the unanswered questions in your life until you are ready for the answers.

2,180

- What have I done today to recognize someone else's leadership?
- What have I tried today that I thought might not work, but I tried it anyway?
- What did I do today to make it more likely someone would learn something?
- What have I done today to make it more likely someone else will reach a goal?
- How did I elevate instead of escalate today?
- What did I do today to be good to myself?

Six questions: two designed to add value to the lives of other people; two designed to drive actions that add value to my life; two designed to add value to both. If I'm disciplined about answering all six of these questions each day (I often fail, but tomorrow is Day One), I'll add over 2,000 moments of impact tied to my core values each year: 2,180 to be exact. Add 2,000 moments of impact to your life and the lives of the people around you and your relationships get better, your career gets better, and your life gets better.

With a phone and laptop, I can answer all six questions faster than I can empty my email inbox each day. For years, however, I prioritized answering my email over deliberately planning to live the values I cared about the most: my leadership was scattershot and unconscious, not planned and deliberate. The Day One leadership process changed that.

These questions are about setting expectations for yourself: if you don't make clear what you expect from yourself and consistently demonstrate behavior that lives up to those expectations, no one cares what you expect from them and no one is going to deliver it.

The creation, sharing, and the disciplined execution of these questions take leadership from theory to execution. It makes core values more than words you use but cannot define, let alone consistently act upon. It drives action.

I've had a lot of pushback over the years on the importance of this process. I've been told it's too soft and too "touchy-feely." I've been asked, "Do you know how smart I am?" or "Do you know how much money I've made?" Most commonly I hear, "Yeah, I can understand how this would be nice to do, but I'm a busy person and I have deliverables, and my bosses don't accept 'I'm living my leadership values' as acceptable results."

So, let me be clear: you can be incredibly accomplished

without doing this. You can be wildly talented without doing this. You can be intellectually brilliant, remarkably driven, tremendously well compensated, and widely respected without doing this; but you *cannot reach your full capacity for leading yourself or a team of people to peak performance* without consistently stating and living up to a clear set of personal leadership values. Research has shown that personal value clarity is linked to improved pride, performance, commitment, and satisfaction and identifying our core values and the values of those we lead is an underutilized tool in our quest to be our best selves and to bring out the best in others.[8]

Leadership is making one big decision to make a series of consistent positive small decisions each day. In Part III, I will take you through the process of operationalizing leadership values in your life by surfacing the values most important to you, defining them, and creating action-oriented questions that will help you live them each day.

In short, we will start to figure out what your personal Day One needs to look like.

Five Ways You Can Embody *Self-Respect* Today (on Day One)

1. Forgive.
2. Put your favorite candy in the cupholder of your car. At some point after a rough day your future self will want to high-five your current self.
3. Say no. A "friendtor" named Joann Lim once told me, "A respectful no is better than a half-assed yes."
4. Ask yourself, "What is my fake leg?" Once again, tell a friend your answer and ask them to hold you accountable for taking it off.
5. Reach out to someone you wish was still in your life to say/hear "I'm sorry."

Questions You Can Ask to Operationalize *Self-Respect*:

- What did I do today to be good to myself?
- How was I my own best friend today?
- What did I do today to prioritize my own needs?
- How did I plant future happiness today?

PART III

Defining the Things You Want to Define You

FOURTEEN

Identifying Your Own Key Values

Now It's All About You

Identify your core leadership values. Define clearly what they mean. Embed them into your life through daily action-oriented questions. That's where you start on Day One. That's how each of us can create the foundation of a leadership of which we are all capable and to which we should all commit.

If you got to start over and build yourself into the leader you hope to be, the actions driven by your key values would be your nonnegotiable commitments on Day One: the foundation of your leadership. Building that foundation takes time, commitment, and repetition.

How do you identify the values to operationalize in your life and create a list of questions that impact you as profoundly as the six that have changed my life? That's what the rest of this book is all about.

Your Three Assignments

Surfacing your key leadership values requires a little homework, it can't be done in your head. Your own list of key values and questions will emerge through three assignments:

1. The Three Key Values Hypothetical
2. Your Edge of the Bed Advice
3. Your Best and Your Worst

Assignment 1—The Three Key Values Hypothetical

You use your core values to pass judgment on yourself and others. Identifying those values is essential to understanding who you are and defining who you want to be, and the *Three Key Values Hypothetical* is a first step. Here's how you put it to work.

1. Consider the following hypothetical:

   Imagine I have someone follow you around for thirty days out of your life. It could be any thirty days, and you have no idea who is following you. This individual sees every interaction of which you are a part: public and private, as well as online and virtual. They see how you interact with people you love, people that you cannot stand, and people you barely know (such as members of the service industry).

   At the end of those thirty days, imagine I asked that person: "What three values does this individual [meaning you] stand for above all others? What three values would you say play the biggest role in influencing their decisions and determining their behavior?"

If you have been the woman/man that you *hope* to be during those thirty days, what three values do you hope that person identifies?

2. Identify and write down the three values upon which you decide. Here's a sample list to assist in the process. It's by no means exhaustive, but I've found it helpful.

Accountability	Forgiveness
Adaptability	Fun
Adventure	Generosity
Authenticity	Gratitude
Autonomy	Growth
Balance	Happiness
Class	Health
Collaboration	Humility
Courage	Impact
Creativity	Innovation
Curiosity	Integrity
Decisiveness	Kindness
Discipline	Love
Drive	Loyalty
Empathy	Mastery
Empowerment	Mindfulness
Fairness	Open-mindedness
Faith	Passion
Family	Perseverance

Positivity	Self-respect
Rationality	Service
Relationships	Tradition
Resilience	Vision
Respect	Vulnerability
Self-awareness	

3. Imagine you had to explain each of your three identified values, simply and thoroughly, to an intelligent person who had never heard the word before. Write down the three definitions you create (start with *a commitment to...*).

No doubt you have more than three values to which you aspire, but it's good to focus on three priority values to begin. Put them aside for now and we'll return to them later.

Assignment 2—Your Edge of the Bed Advice

Everyone has wisdom to share: regardless of your age, experience, level of education, or economic status, everyone has learned from their experiences. The lessons learned from what you've *done*, rather than what you've been told, constitute your wisdom.

In the chapter on the value of growth, I introduced the Edge of the Bed Question:

Imagine it's the final night your son or daughter is living in your house (this may require imagining you have a son or a daughter). Tomorrow they're off to school, or getting married, or moving away to start their first job.

You're walking by their room and they call you in. As you sit down on the edge of their bed, they look up at you and ask: "Mom/Dad, what's your best life advice? What single insight has most contributed to your happiness?"

What would you tell them?

This question has a drawback: it puts a lot of pressure on people! Asked for a single insight that has most contributed to their happiness, people start looking for some transcendent truth and fail to share some of their most useful wisdom.

My friend Hamza (he of "elevate don't escalate" fame) changed the way I utilize the Edge of the Bed Question when he blogged "25 Lessons I Have Learned in 25 Years" on his twenty-fifth birthday. Having pulled a ton of insight from his post I endeavored to create my own list on my birthday a few weeks later. No longer having to distill all my successes, failures, lessons, heartbreaks, and moments of both insight and idiocy into a single lesson, I discovered the assignment was far more fun and significantly more useful as a tool in the Day One process. So yes, you're going to have to create a list of thirty yourself. Here's a sample list to get the juices flowing:

Sample Edge of the Bed Advice

1. Stop saying "it's complicated" when it really isn't.
2. You must be the love of your own life.
3. Don't obsess about five-year plans: focus on creating five-year momentum.
4. There are a lot more Rosalines out there than Juliets.

5. Both Romeo and Juliet end up dead at the end of that story. Love doesn't conquer all. It does, however, have a quality winning percentage. Love is LeBron James. Adjust expectations accordingly.

6. Not starting something when you know it will make your life better is a form of giving up.

7. Feel free to dismiss the judgments of anyone who is not as happy as you are.

8. "Never give in—never, never, never, never, in nothing great or small, large or petty, never give in except to convictions of honor and good sense." Remember the end of that quotation as well as the first three words.

9. The dog that's running up to you now is not the one that bit you when you were eight.

10. There are three things in life you must have, or one day you're going to miss out on a cool opportunity:
    • The ability to drive stick
    • An up-to-date passport
    • Two saved-up vacation days

11. The words "I love you" are wonderful. Actions that demonstrate "I love you" are better.

12. If you've always wanted to see them perform, go see them perform. Now.

13. Happiness is when most of the things you *have to* do every day are things that you want to do.

14. Your emotions aren't the problem, judging yourself for having them is the problem.

15. Everything you want in the world is on the other side of something shitty.

16. The higher the speed limit on the road, the more boring it is.
17. Money isn't everything, but debt can be. Save.
18. Remember that life has armed you with will and determination...and grace, too.
19. Don't hate your body, but don't lie to yourself when it's unhealthy.
20. It doesn't get easier, you just get better at it.
21. Only hurt people hurt others.
22. There is nothing on earth that cannot be made better by sleep and a shower.
23. Success is feeling like you're enough even when you're going after something more.
24. Sometimes the best way to shine is to reflect the light of others. Just ask the moon.
25. It's better to be decisive than certain in life. The former is possible, the latter rarely is.
26. Joy is the sexiest thing on the planet.
27. Great stories aren't about what you did, they're about what you were afraid of while you did it.
28. Your values determine how you judge yourself. Your priorities determine how you behave. Work to align the two.
29. In politics, the creation of fear is used to win. In leadership, the removal of fear is used to succeed. Be a leader.
30. I've never seen a baby squirrel, but that doesn't mean they don't exist.

Creating Your Own Edge of the Bed Advice

An essential step in identifying your core values is to *create a list of your own thirty pieces of Edge of the Bed Advice.* Your list is not a ranking: your insights need not appear in any particular order—write them down as they come to you. What's important is you reflect on the sum of your experiences and identify lessons that could add value to others. Don't feel your list needs to be created in one sitting. Take some time to reflect and use these tips to help put it together:

- What wisdom have you received from others that has consistently made your life better? Pay it forward! Originality isn't nearly as important as effectiveness in this exercise.

- Think back to the last few times something blew up in your face and you thought, "Damn it, I know better than that!" What principle or piece of wisdom did you ignore in that situation?

- List five of the happiest times in your life. Is there a common thread weaving those five times together: something you did; something you avoided doing?

- Create a note on your phone labeled "My Wisdom." Take a few minutes each day over coffee, in the shower, or heading to work to ask, "What's something I know to be true about _____?" Finish that sentence with any number of these:

Disappointment	Failure	Family
Fear	Friendship	Happiness
Health	Leadership	Love
Myself	Stress	Work

- Ask others what they would include on their lists. Your wisdom is often best unlocked when hearing that of others.

Assignment 3—Your Best and Your Worst

This assignment can be a tough one: it gives you the opportunity to celebrate times when you feel you were at your best, but also requires you reflect on moments you may prefer not to think about.

Reflect on your life and identify four situations:

- Two situations in which you behaved in a way that still makes you very proud or happy. When you think of these situations you feel you truly reflected the person you hope to be.
- Two situations in which you behaved in a way that still upsets/disappoints you. When you think of these situations you feel you failed to live up to the expectations you set for yourself. As difficult as it might be it is generally best to focus on those moments where you were most deeply disappointed.

To do this well you must be open and vulnerable with perhaps your toughest audience: yourself. Most of us are hesitant to celebrate what makes us great—we'd rather be humble. However, humility isn't denying what makes you extraordinary; it's recognizing what makes you extraordinary doesn't make you *better* than anyone else. Be willing to push through the discomfort of patting yourself on the back and truly explore the moments in your life of which you are proudest.

On the other side of the coin, while we often dwell on the experiences we deeply regret, we rarely analyze them. We attach emotions of shame, fear, and grief to an experience and rarely move past those emotions to reflect on how and why our most negative experiences occurred. What did we do wrong? How exactly did we fail ourselves? Push through those negative emotions and summarize what actually happened, not just how you feel about it.

When you try to do these assignments, you'll find it's a lot easier to remember your negative experiences. Don't allow yourself to feel frustrated, angry, or ashamed of that. Negative experiences imprint themselves on our brains much more powerfully than do positive ones.

Reverse-Engineering Values

Once you've completed the Three Key Values Hypothetical, your list of Edge of the Bed Advice and identified two instances of pride and two instances of disappointment, it's time to surface your values.

Leave the Three Key Values Hypothetical aside for a moment and let's look at your Edge of the Bed Advice. That list has emerged from your *lived experiences*: things that worked and things that didn't; moments that made you happy and those that caused pain; actions that empowered those around you and actions that set people back. Trace each insight back: you'll find almost every one of them was a lesson you learned because of something you *did* (or failed to do).

These are the lessons learned from the life you've lived, not some idealized version of yourself. As such, that list represents core values that are important to you. Look at each insight on your list—with each one you are saying:

"If you take this piece of advice to heart, you'll do a better job of living the value(s) of _____."

At the root of each of your thirty insights are one or more foundational values. By creating your list of insights first and *then* looking for the foundational values, you can identify which values are most important to you in an indirect but extremely revealing way. Essentially, I'm going to ask you to "reverse-engineer" a list of key values using your list of insights. For each one, take a moment and say to yourself:

"Complete this sentence: if someone was to take this piece of advice to heart and live by it each day, they would do a better job embodying [INSERT VALUE HERE]."

Complete that sentence by considering the story behind each of your insights: What does it teach? What pitfalls would it help someone avoid? What new perspectives might it create for the person who receives it? Here are some examples using the sample Edge of the Bed Advice provided earlier:

Stop saying "it's complicated" when it really isn't.
Years ago, a friend called me to tell me he had fallen hard for a woman and that she had the same feelings for him.

"That's great!" I said. "So, you guys are together?"

"Well no," he replied. "It's complicated."

"How so?" I asked.

"Well, she's dating my best friend," he answered.

That's not complicated. It's not complicated if you can explain it in five words. What's complicated is getting what you want and being the person who you want to be. Being a leader means making decisions based on what you believe to be right rather than what brings the most rewards or avoids the most consequences

If someone were to take this piece of advice to heart and live by it each day, they would do a better job embodying the values of courage, self-respect, *and* class.

You must be the love of your own life.

Another gem from Paralympian Stephanie Dixon. A friend had invited me to speak to his class of eighth-grade students, almost all of whom were teen girls. Being a little out of my wheelhouse demographic-wise, I asked Steph what advice she'd give a roomful of young women.

"Tell them they have to be the love of their own life," she replied, and she lives that sentiment: around her ring finger, in the spot often reserved for a wedding ring, she has tattooed the word "enough."

"I married myself," she told me. "It's to remind me that I am enough. I don't need a ring from someone else to be complete.

"You should be the most committed to the person you spend your entire life with," she finished. "Tell them to never compromise their commitment to themselves to try to attract or please someone else."

This insight points to the need to recognize your autonomy and have enough self-awareness and respect to never settle in your relationships.

If someone were to take this piece of advice to heart and live by it each day, they would do a better job embodying the values of self-respect, self-awareness, *and* autonomy.

Don't obsess about five-year plans. Focus on creating five-year momentum.

This is another insight from my man Mustafa. Beyond the wisdom he had shared with me on our day together, he and his fellow drivers provided me with a memory to last a lifetime. As the day wound to a close, I asked him what it took to be a great "dune driver."

"Resisting the urge to go too slowly," he replied. "Driving in the dunes is like finding your way through life: there's going to be an urge to go slowly to try to be safe. Unfortunately, being safe and going slowly are not always the same thing."

"They're not?" I asked. "Doesn't going a little more slowly mean you have more time to react to things? More time to see problems coming and create plans to deal with them? Doesn't it give you a little more control?"

Mustafa shook his head. "That's our instinct, I know, but in the sand going too slowly takes away your control. If you don't have enough speed and momentum, your choices are taken from you and your environment controls where you go. You can turn the wheel all you want but your fate is with the sand. It will slide you or flip you the way it chooses. But if you build up the right amount of speed, you can have complete control, though you must always be cautious to build up only the speed necessary to generate control and choices. Speed up too much and once again you are no longer in charge of your own movements. You may get to choose the direction, but you won't be able to adjust beyond that."

He took a long drink of water and thought for a moment. "Here in the desert, like in life, your momentum is what gives you your choices. Too slow and your environment takes control from you, too fast and you take it from yourself.

"Momentum is crucial," he went on. "When I first took over the company, I was asked often for my five-year-plan. The problem with plans is they change how you look at opportunities. If you focus on plans, you'll evaluate every opportunity for how well it fits into your plan and those that don't are often dismissed without too much analysis. If you evaluate every opportunity that presents itself by how much momentum it creates, every opportunity gets fair consideration, even the unexpected ones."

He smiled it me. "A long time ago I stopped worrying about five-year plans. All I care about now is generating five-year momentum."

If someone were to take this piece of advice to heart and live by it each day, they would do a better job embodying the value of adaptability.

There are a lot more Rosalines out there than Juliets.
Rosaline is the woman over whom Romeo is pining at the beginning of *Romeo and Juliet*. We never see her or hear from her directly, but according to Romeo she's all he could ever want in a woman and he doubts he can go on living without her. Until, of course, he meets Juliet.

There have been an awful lot of things in my life I've been utterly convinced I must have in order to be happy, only to be tremendously grateful I didn't end up getting them. This insight aims to illustrate that most of the things we'll desire in our lives we probably can probably live without and we should bear that in mind when we deal with the hurt or anger that comes with not getting them.

If someone were to take this piece of advice to heart and live by it each day, they would do a better job embodying the values of resilience *and* perseverance.

Both Romeo and Juliet end up dead at the end of that story. Love doesn't conquer all. It does, however, have a quality winning percentage. Love is LeBron James. Adjust expectations accordingly.

You can't truly embrace love until you accept its limitations. This insight points to two important truths: love is a powerful force that will make your life better, and sometimes it will end, often painfully. Embrace love, enter into it rationally with your eyes open, and build the resilience necessary to deal with it ending.

If someone were to take this piece of advice to heart and live by it each day, they would do a better job embodying the values of love, rationality, *and* resilience.

Move through your list of Edge of the Bed Insights and apply this process: for each item on your list identify one to three foundational values. Use the tally sheet in Appendix III on page 247 to track how many times each value appears.

The biggest challenge with this process is that people generally lack a "value lexicon": a list of values from which to choose. To make this process easier I've included a list of sample values and definitions in Appendix II. For ease of reference, here's that list of the values once again:

Accountability

Adaptability

Adventure

Authenticity

Autonomy

Balance

Class

Collaboration

Courage

Creativity

Curiosity

Decisiveness

Discipline

Drive

Empathy

Empowerment

Fairness

Faith

Family

Forgiveness

Fun

Generosity

Gratitude

Growth

Happiness

Health

Humility

Impact

Innovation

Integrity

Kindness

Love

Loyalty

Mastery

Mindfulness

Open-mindedness

Passion

Perseverance

Positivity

Rationality

Relationships

Resilience

Respect

Self-awareness

Self-respect

Service

Tradition

Vision

Vulnerability

Don't hesitate to use values you don't find here as you identify the foundations of your Edge of the Bed insights. Once you've gone through your list and tallied up your results you can move on to the next section.

Surfacing Values

I reverse-engineered the foundational values for the sample Edge of the Bed Advice, identifying one to three foundational values for each insight, and identified thirty different values. Some of those thirty appeared more frequently than others:

Self-respect 10	Humility 2
Resilience 7	Forgiveness 2
Courage 7	Adaptability 2
Perseverance 5	Love 2
Rationality 4	Faith 1
Discipline 4	Service 1
Adventure 4	Collaboration 1
Self-awareness 4	Mindfulness 1
Class 3	Balance 1
Happiness 3	Empathy 1
Impact 3	Mastery 1
Fun 2	Innovation 1
Empowerment 2	Creativity 1
Passion 2	Autonomy 1
Decisiveness 2	

Once you have done the same for your Edge of the Bed Advice, turn to your review of the four positive and negative situations in your life. You identified each of those four situations, good and bad, because of how you acted in relation to your core values. The two situations you identified as generating pride did so because you embodied a value or values that were of great importance to you. The disappointment you feel about the other two situations exists due to a violation of deeply held personal values. It's quite possible you have no idea what those values are but they're among the most important you hold. These four situations emerged as particularly important in your life, so the values that drove them are tied deeply to your identity.

Examine the two situations of which you are proudest and ask yourself: *What values did my behavior embody in this situation?* Write them down.

Turn now to the moments of which you are ashamed and ask yourself: *What are the values I violated with my behavior in this situation?* Write them down.

When a value is identified in the Best and Worst assignment it deserves more weight on your tally sheet than those identified in the Edge of the Bed assignment. For demonstration purposes, let's say you determined the following six values were embodied or violated in your Best and Worst assignment:

- Self-respect
- Courage
- Discipline
- Adventure
- Perseverance
- Decisiveness

If the sample Edge of the Bed list was your own, you'd add two additional tallies to each of those six values:

Self-respect 10 + 2 = 12   **Perseverance 5 + 2 = 7**
Courage 7 + 2 = 9   Resilience 7

Discipline 4 + 2 = 6	Adaptability 2
Adventure 4 + 2 = 6	Love 2
Rationality 4	Faith 1
Self-awareness 4	Service 1
Class 3	Collaboration 1
Happiness 3	Mindfulness 1
Impact 3	Balance 1
Fun 2	Empathy 1
Empowerment 2	Mastery 1
Passion 2	Innovation 1
Decisiveness 2 + 2 = 4	Creativity 1
Humility 2	Autonomy 1
Forgiveness 2	

In this demonstration of the process you could identify four to six values to operationalize into daily behaviors:

- Self-respect
- Courage
- Perseverance
- Resilience
- Discipline
- Adventure

There is no hard-and-fast rule as to how many should be identified for operationalization, use your discretion once you complete the assignments. I suggest no fewer than three and no more than six. Begin the next section once you've finished surfacing your core values through this process.

Value Perception vs. Value Reality

Compare the values you've surfaced through this process to the three values you identified in the first assignment: the Three Key Values Hypothetical. Do they align? If so, congratulations, you are part of a small group whose perception of your values matches the reality of your actions. The remainder of this book will help you embed those values more consistently into your daily behavior.

For most people the three values they identify as most important in the first assignment are not consistent with those that surface through the experience-based assignments. That's not to say the values you identified in the first assignment are not desirable and important, just that they may not be an accurate reflection of what truly drives you.

It's essential to go through exercises that surface your values rather than simply try to identify them through reflection. If you use your values as criteria for decision making, those decisions will be hard to live with if you fail to use the proper criteria. Imagine you're facing a difficult decision and remember the adage "Do what the person I want to be would do." You hold up the options available next to what you believe are your core values and it becomes clear that one of those options is more consistent with those values than the other options. Unfortunately, it's an option that brings with it serious consequences—social, emotional, and financial. You choose that option anyway, secure in the knowledge you've stayed true to your core values. The decision is not popular with your friends or coworkers: it costs you a promotion (or perhaps even a job) and perhaps ends a friendship. However, you take solace in the fact that it was consistent with the things that matter to you the most.

Now, consider the possibility you were wrong: the values you used as the criteria for that decision are *not* in fact those most important to you. Five years from now, as you look back on the decision and try to come to grips with its consequences, it's possible you'll feel it was a mistake.

We are willing to accept the consequences that come from staying true to our values as long as those values are truly the ones most important to us. If they are not, we tend to continually regret and resent the decisions we've made and the consequences they bring. It's essential the values you choose to operationalize on Day One are in fact the ones most consistent with the leader you hope to be. Make sure you go through the assignments and determine if your value perception matches your value reality.

Summary—How to Surface Your Key Values

1. Create a list of your *Edge of the Bed Advice*: Thirty insights about life and work that you feel lead to happiness and success.

2. Summarize two situations in your life where you are extremely proud of how you behaved.

3. Summarize two situations in your life where you are ashamed of how you behaved.

4. Identify each insight's foundational values by completing the sentence: "If I take this insight to heart, I will do a better job of living the values of [INSERT VALUES HERE]." Identify one to four values per insight.

   - Track each value as it is identified on the tally sheet found in Appendix III. Place one tally each time a value appears.

5. For the two situations in your life where you are proud of how you behaved, ask yourself, "Which key value or values did I truly embody in this situation?"

   - Track each value on the tally sheet but place *two* tallies each time a value is identified.

6. For the two situations in your life where you are ashamed of how you behaved, ask yourself, "Which key value or values did I violate in this situation?"

   - Track each value on the tally sheet but place *two* tallies each time a value is identified.

7. You should have between 34 and approximately 100 different tallies on the sheet. Identify which three to six values stand out from the rest. These are the values you will operationalize though action-driving questions.

FIFTEEN

Creating Your Own Questions

What Makes an Effective Question?

Let's return to that first value I ever aimed to operationalize through this process:

Impact: A commitment to creating moments that cause people to feel better for having interacted with you.

I live that value every day by finding an answer to this question by the time I go to bed:

"What have I done today to recognize someone else's leadership?"

That question was created to have specific characteristics that any question used in this process must have:

1. To answer it you have to *do* something.

An action-driving question cannot be a yes–no question. Yes–no questions allow you to lie to yourself about whether you've answered them. Asking yourself, Did I have impact today? allows you to say, "Sure I did," without having to identify any specific action you took to do so. Asking *Did I recognize someone else's leadership today?* allows you to say yes, but asking **What have I done today** *to recognize someone else's leadership?* demands you specify when and how you did it. Being required to specify the when and how makes it more likely the question will drive you to take at least one distinct, conscious, deliberate act designed to embody a value that's important to you.

The simplest way to make sure that a question will drive action is to start the question in one of two ways:

- "How did I…" or
- "What did I do today to…"

"How did I recognize someone else's leadership today?"

"What did I do today that might not work but I tried it anyway?"

"How did I make it more likely someone else would move closer to a goal today?"

"What did I do today to make it more likely someone will learn something?"

I can't answer any of those questions without pointing to a specific act I accomplished or tried to accomplish—none of them can be answered with a simple yes or no. You'll notice, however, that even though those questions are supposed to help me embody impact, courage, empowerment, and growth, the actual words "impact," "courage," "empowerment," and "growth" don't appear in any of the questions.

That's the second characteristic of a good action-oriented question:

2. It shouldn't include the actual value in the question.

Asking *What did I do today to empower someone else?* or *How did I embody growth today?* doesn't keep people motivated over the long term. A better strategy is to examine each value's definition and ask, "What does living up to this definition actually look like?" Create a list of specific behaviors or actions you'd associate with living that value and pick one as the basis for your question.

To illustrate: if courage is defined as "a commitment to taking action in the face of potential loss," consider what specific behaviors would live up to that commitment. You could do any of the following:

- Challenge the way something has always been done.
- Try something you've never tried before.
- Attempt something at which you've already failed.
- Be open about something of which you're scared.
- Set a goal that's more ambitious than you've accomplished previously.

Any one of those behaviors can embody courage, but listing them gives you the opportunity to consider creative combinations and generate more effective questions. For instance, "What have I done today that might not work, but I tried it anyway?"

Let's apply the same approach to the value of impact once again. Here are a few examples of what kind of specific behaviors would make someone walk away from you feeling better about the interaction:

- Say something kind about how they look.
  - Say something kind about someone they care about.
  - Give them something they might want or need.
  - Try to say something that would make them smile or laugh.
  - Point out something they did that impressed you.

Focus on the final behavior—pointing out something they did that impressed you. Now imagine you ran a leadership development program—by what kind of behavior would you be most impressed? You guessed it—this is exactly how we came up with the first ever action-driving question in the Day One process: *What have I done today to recognize someone else's leadership?* We took a behavior consistent with our value and specialized it for our specific needs.

Avoid creating a question that includes the value. Instead, look at the definitions for your core values and list specific acts that satisfy those definitions. You'll find it helps you create great questions.

3. There's flexibility in how it can be answered.

The more ways you can answer an action-driving question the more likely it will become a consistent part of your personal leadership culture. For instance, let's say that efficiency was a value central to your identity. *What did I do today to keep my office neat?* certainly meets the first two criteria of an effective question, but it breaks down on this one. That question can only be answered a few ways and can only be answered at work. You won't have a lot of variety of choices over the long haul and you'll probably stop being excited about answering the question.

Try shifting that question to *What did I do today to make my life more efficient?* You'd be able to come up with something new every day at both home *and* work: you could hang a new key ring near the door so you don't have to look for your keys or buy extra phone charging cords so there's always one waiting for you at your desk and in the rooms in which you spend the most time. On the days a creative idea eludes you, you can always go back to "I tidied up my office" as your answer.

Answering your questions must involve doing something specific, but your questions need to be broad enough that *something* could be different every day and fit neatly into your life. Any plan that works only when you have extra time or are having a good day isn't going to be an effective plan long term.

To recap, an effective question:

1. Cannot be answered yes or no—it must demand you identify what you did and how you did it.
2. Should not include the actual value in the question.
3. Must provide flexibility in how it can be answered.

In the next chapter you'll have the chance to practice using these characteristics to identify a quality question.

SIXTEEN

Practice Identifying a Good Question

In the previous chapter we identified the key characteristics of an effective action-driving question:

1. It cannot be answered yes or no—it must demand you identify what you did and how you did it.
2. It shouldn't include the actual value in the question.
3. It must provide flexibility in how it can be answered.

Identifying quality action-driving questions is a new skill for almost everyone (hey, it's Day One!), so this chapter will give you the opportunity to practice.

We'll start with generosity: a commitment to identifying, seeking out, or creating opportunities to give more than is required of yourself and your resources.

Using that definition of generosity, and keeping in mind the characteristics of a good question, consider the following questions and identify which would be most effective in driving behaviors associated with generosity:

- Was I generous today?
- How did I give more than I "had to" today?
- Did I give something away today?
- When did I give something away I could have easily kept for myself?

Let's look at each option a little more closely to evaluate its potential effectiveness as an action-driving question.

Was I generous today? This question fails to live up to two standards for a great action-oriented question: it can be answered with a yes or no and it uses the value in the question itself.

How did I give more than I "had to" today? This question meets all the criteria of what makes an effective action-driver: it cannot be answered yes or no, it doesn't include the value in the question, and it can be answered any number of ways.

Did I give something away today? Giving something away could be an indication of generosity, but this question can be answered with a simple yes or no, allowing you to answer it without identifying a specific moment when you demonstrated generosity. A slight tweak to *What did I do today to give something away?* would greatly increase its effectiveness.

When did I give something away I could have easily kept for myself? This is another question that meets all the criteria for an effective action-driving question.

Two of those four questions stand out as effective at driving actions each day: "How did I give more than I 'had to' today?" and "When did I give away something I could have easily kept for myself?" Neither of them can be answered with a yes or no and both provide for a variety of potential answers: you could identify an instance where you gave away money, or time, or support, or expertise in any number of ways.

Let's try it again with a different value, *gratitude*: a commitment to seeking out or creating opportunities to celebrate positive things.

Using that definition of gratitude, and again keeping in mind the characteristics of a good question, consider the following questions as potential avenues to operationalize gratitude:

- How did I let someone know they were appreciated today?
- What did I do today to acknowledge something good in my life?
- Did I say "thank you" to someone today?
- What are three things for which I'm grateful today?

Again, let's examine the four questions a little more closely:

How did I let someone know they were appreciated today?
What did I do today to acknowledge something good in my life?

These are both effective questions, and avoid some of the issues inherent in the other two.

Did I say "thank you" to someone today? Saying "thank you" is a great way to recognize positive things, but this question can be answered with a yes or a no. It could be adapted into a more effective question by asking, *What did I do today to thank someone?* or *How did I let someone know I appreciated something they did for me today?*

What are three things for which I'm grateful today? Taking the time to reflect on the things for which you are grateful is an amazing exercise and I encourage you to do it. However, creating that list would be better used to answer one of the other questions as opposed to serving as a question itself. You also want to avoid using the actual value in your question.

As you make answering action-oriented questions a more consistent part of your days, you'll become better at creating questions for yourself. You'll start to learn which questions generate the most options, fit best into your life, and get you most excited each day. Be patient, you'll get better at it, but even the first few days will yield positive results.

SEVENTEEN

Putting the Day One
Process into Action

Put the Day One process into action gradually and systematically beginning with a single value surfaced through the previous exercises. I suggest the value that received the most tallies on your score sheet, but you can choose any that were surfaced as important to you. The key is to choose the value that for whatever reason resonates most strongly with you right now. This is the value that will serve as the foundation for your Day One. It is this value you will work on operationalizing over the next month by ensuring you ask and answer an action-oriented question.

Create your own action-oriented question using the process in the previous chapters, or you can simply choose one of the sample questions provided for each value in Appendix II starting on page 233.

Once you've created or attached a question to each of your chosen values, you may feel the urge to try to work in more than one question per day right away. It's crucial in the early stages of this process that you focus on just a single question to add to your life. Adopt the mindset that each new day of your life must be earned by passing a test for which you've been given the questions in advance.

Make a notification in your phone or in your scheduling app: have the question pop up each morning, at lunch, and toward the end of the day as a reminder that it *must* be answered. Create a note on your phone, a folder on your computer, or carry a notebook to journal exactly how you answer the question each day.

After thirty days, add the second value and associated question to your daily commitment. Continue to answer the first question as you move forward. Add another one of your core values and its associated question every thirty days. Continue to journal how you answer them each day. It won't take long before you'll start to see a major impact, and on days when you're feeling like you don't matter, you can open your journal and be reminded that the evidence says otherwise.

At this point you've taken the steps necessary to embrace the "This Is Day One" philosophy: you've identified the core values you wish to drive you and you've created a strategy to ensure you start living up to them each day. What you need now is practice and discipline to keep asking and answering your first question for a month so that you can add your second, then third, and so on.

There will be days when you're not successful and that's okay. The great thing about looking at each day as Day One is there's no shame in doing something poorly on your first day. This process allows you to forgive yourself when you're less than the person you want to be and keeps you from getting too full of yourself when you've been doing a good job.

Consistency is key: ordinary acts performed with extraordinary consistency change worlds. Make no mistake, you're a world changer. Don't be intimidated: remember there is no world, simply 7 billion understandings of it. Every time you change one person's understanding of the world—be it an understanding of how many people care about them, of what they're capable, or how powerful an agent for change they can be in this world or in their own life—you've changed the whole world. That's not beneath you and it's not beyond you.

I've focused on specific behaviors and the power of individual moments throughout this book, but focusing on Day One doesn't mean this approach does not provide a cumulative benefit. You recommit on Day One, you don't restart. Each new Day One builds on the one before.

Sometimes this cumulative impact is imperceptible, and we fail to see how our commitments are truly improving our lives and the lives of others. Should you ever find yourself wondering if your daily leadership is really making a difference, I encourage you to think about one final story.

A man approached me once saying he'd wanted to share something with me ever since he'd watched my "lollipop moment" video online. His story moved me so much I asked him to tell it twice. I share it here in his voice:

> I grew up on a farm, and then went to school at a tiny liberal arts college in a small town. The first time I ever lived in a city was when I got my first job here in Chicago. On my way to work my first day, I stopped at a red light and saw

my first ever homeless person. He was moving between the cars with a coffee cup, hoping for change. The problem was, I had no idea how to behave in that situation: I didn't have any money and I didn't know if he'd get mad or what, so I ended up panicking a little. I started looking all over the car for any money at all—the center console, under the passenger seat, in the back. When I finally looked up, there was the homeless guy, looking at me through my window with a really amused look on his face.

"Hey, New Guy!" he shouted. "Don't worry about it! If you don't have any money you just smile, wave, and tell me, 'Not today, my friend.' It's all good."

He leaned a little closer to the window and told me, "But I can tell you're new here, so let me give you a little piece of advice: don't let this city beat you down. If it hasn't beat me—and it never will—you shouldn't let it beat you! Deal?"

"Yes sir," I stammered. The guy burst out laughing and just walked off.

The next day, he was there at the same intersection on my way to work. When he saw me he yelled, "New Guy! City beat you down yet?"

I was like, "Uh...no? You?"

He gave me this huge smile and said, "I told ya: never!" Then I gave him a buck and he wished me a good day and just kept moving on down the road.

This became what the two of us did every day. I found out his name was Larry, and I'd save whatever the change was from my morning coffee stop for him. Every day when he'd see me he'd yell, "New Guy! City beat you down yet?" and I'd say, "Nah, Larry, you?" He'd always reply "I told ya: never!," take the money, wish me a good day, and move on.

So, this goes on for about a year, and then one day when I pulled up and held out the dollar, he shakes his head and doesn't take it.

"You know, my man," he said, "hundreds of people drive by me every day and won't even make eye contact. You've given me money pretty much every single day I've ever seen you. You know what? You've done your share. Keep it today, we'll pick it up again tomorrow."

I don't really know why, but I reached into my wallet, grabbed everything I had—it was about sixty bucks—and just held it out to him.

"How about today I do their share instead?" I asked.

It was weird, because he didn't take the money right away. He just stares at me for most of the light, and then right before it turns green, he takes it, nods, and then just walks off. No "have a good day," nothing.

But we kept up our "has the city beat you down" thing every day and then about two years after that time with the sixty bucks, I was driving by that intersection with a woman in the passenger seat. It was only our third date, but I was really into her, and all I was thinking about was not screwing it all up.

So, we stop at the light, and Larry sees me and starts heading over. I'm a little nervous, because I have no idea what my date is going to think of my homeless buddy. Larry goes right over to her window and leans down and smiles at her.

"Hey," he said, "my name's Larry. I don't know if that guy over there is the only person in the world who knows that, but I will tell you he is the only person who has asked my name in the past four years. You should know, though, since I first saw him scared out of his mind at this intersection three years ago, he's given me exactly $1,521.68. One day he gave me sixty bucks. It made me feel like a friend instead of a charity case. You should know you're out with a very special man...don't screw it up." Then he walked off.

The night I asked her to marry me, my wife told me that was the moment she knew she was going to say yes.

That $1,521.68 wasn't handed over as part of a conscious process; the man telling the story wasn't trying to live up to some personal leadership philosophy. It's an example of the simple but unconscious leadership you are already demonstrating every day. Day One leadership is about being more conscious and deliberate about creating those moments, even if you don't feel the momentum they are creating or see the impact they are having.

This book has talked an awful lot about questions, but if I was going to send you out on Day One with the training-wheel version of how to generate more moments of leadership every day, I'd boil it down to these two:

1. *What is my dollar?*
2. *Who is my Larry?*

Your dollar could be a smile, an act of generosity, or perhaps even asking the name of someone panhandling on your way to work. Your Larry could be a friend, mentor, student, or a stranger with whom you cross paths. You'll often find that in looking to give you get back a lot more—that's the cycle of leadership and it's well above the "great line."

I stayed in touch with Jimmy and Earl via email after my train trip. They didn't spend a lot of time online, but every now and then I'd receive a note from one of them. About two years after we met, I got an email from Earl: Jimmy had passed away a couple of weeks before, and Earl thought I might enjoy reading the obituary that Jimmy had chosen to write for himself. His final line reminds us how important it is to ask ourselves what it is we want to stand for as we aim to change people's understandings of the world:

Discovered on Juno Beach what he was willing to die for. Then lived for it every day of his life.

By now I hope you know what you want to stand for every day. So, start today: on Day One.

EIGHTEEN

What Kind of Day Has It Been?

I started this book to share a process I believed in—a process that began as a way to help university students engage in impactful leadership behaviors on a daily basis. Honestly, I never expected it to be applied more broadly than that. Yet here you are.

I finished this book to keep a promise.

One night about fifteen years ago, I was leaning against a bar with a friend of mine. He was staring across the room, a look of utter contentment on his face as he watched his girlfriend dance. I'd never seen anyone look at someone else quite like that.

"You really love that girl, don't you?" I asked him.

He leaned toward me without taking his eyes off her. "That's not a girl," he said quietly. "That's a unicorn."

I raised an eyebrow and he glanced at me before returning his gaze to the dance floor.

"There are people who will come into your life who are so

magical, so powerful, and so rare that you're never quite the same," he explained. "When someone changes you that way, has that kind of power over you, that's a unicorn."

He looked over at me. "Not everyone gets one. It's a gift if you do."

I didn't think I'd get that gift. Then I met Anastasia.

Anastasia taught me that love isn't passion, it's fascination: a deep, unrelenting, sometimes infuriating fascination with another human being. I was fascinated by her mind, her beauty, how she challenged me, and how every day she managed to give me something I didn't even know I wanted or needed.

On New Year's Day 2017, she made me promise to finish this book.

On January 17 of that year she died by suicide.

That was a Day One for me. Day One as someone left behind.

Treat every day like it's Day One. Doing so will help you forgive yourself for missteps, avoid becoming too full of yourself when you've got momentum, and ensure that every day you do the foundational things necessary for long-term success.

Having shared that philosophy for years, I suddenly found myself on a journey I didn't think I could get through by following my own advice. I could not live that Day One over and over, and I began to question if I could continue to share the philosophy. Like everything else in the aftermath of her death, I had no concept of what my professional future would look like.

The months that followed revealed a powerful truth about the Day One philosophy: it is a road map through uncertainty. There are many times in our lives when we are uncertain about the future: uncertain about our careers, our relationships, our health. When we're not sure what the future holds we often hesitate to act in the present—fearing that if we don't know exactly where we're going, moving forward can be a dangerous mistake. So, we tread water—going through large portions of our lives feeling like we're in a holding pattern and wasting our days waiting for some version of the future to become clearer.

Many hopes for my future were blown apart that January morning, but I continue doing the things I've taught you in this book. I continue to answer the questions this process helped me create because while my future is unclear, it's coming nonetheless, and I will not stop developing the man I want to be when it arrives. Despite my uncertainty, the behaviors the Day One approach have embedded in my life are giving me direction. They're helping me move through a profoundly difficult time and recognize I'm going to be okay even if I don't know how or when.

The Day One philosophy can help you create daily momentum even when you don't know where that momentum will take you. It creates a to-do list for each day of your life—a list of behaviors that will generate positive moments of impact, courage, empowerment, growth, and self-respect that will take you to better places, even if you're unclear exactly where those places might be. It is a tool you too can use to move through uncertainty. To lead yourself and to matter every day.

I started writing this book because I believed in the Day One philosophy. I finished it because now I swear by it. I hope you'll come to swear by it too. I wish you so much more than luck.

Value List and Definitions

Accountability
A commitment to delivering on promises and acknowledging responsibility for the outcomes of your actions

Adaptability
A commitment to changing when necessary

Adventure
A commitment to seeking out new and/or exciting experiences

Authenticity
A commitment to making decisions based on your own beliefs and values rather than the expectations of others

Autonomy
A commitment to seeking independence

Balance

A commitment to pursuing equilibrium in your thoughts, action and being

Class

A commitment to treating people and situations better than they deserve to be treated, even when you have every right not to

Collaboration

A commitment to cooperating with others in the pursuit of goals

Courage

A commitment to taking action when there is a possibility of loss

Creativity

A commitment to generating ideas and behaving in ways that are different from your norm

Curiosity

A commitment to asking questions and seeking answers

Decisiveness

A commitment to taking definitive action

Discipline

A commitment to overcoming distractions

Drive

A commitment to creating or maintaining momentum

Empathy

A commitment to trying to understand and share the experiences and emotions of others

Empowerment

A commitment to acting as a catalyst for the success of others

Fairness

A commitment to equal opportunity

Faith

A commitment to having an absolute trust in something

Family

A commitment to prioritizing the relationships of those you consider family

Forgiveness

A commitment to letting go of negative thoughts and emotions about those who have harmed you (including yourself)

Fun

A commitment to creating, finding, or embracing moments of enjoyment

Generosity

A commitment to identifying, seeking out, or creating opportunities to give more than is required of yourself and your resources

Gratitude

A commitment to honor the good, the bad, and the ugly in your life for the person those experiences helped you become

Growth

A commitment to expanding the capacity to add value

Happiness

A commitment to generating positive emotions

Health

A commitment to engaging in actions that contribute to physical, psychological, emotional, spiritual, and intellectual strength and wellness

Humility

A commitment to recognizing that the things that make you awesome don't make you better than anyone else

Impact

A commitment to creating moments that cause people to walk away feeling as if they are better off for having interacted with you

Innovation

A commitment to challenging and improving the status quo

Integrity

A commitment to using a consistent set of criteria for decision making

Kindness
A commitment to creating moments where someone feels their well-being was your only motivation for doing something.

Love
A commitment to creating emotional connections without conditions

Loyalty
A commitment to honoring your connections and commitments

Mastery
A commitment to seeking continuous improvement

Mindfulness
A commitment to being conscious, aware, and engaged in any given moment

Open-mindedness
A commitment to exploring the validity of new ideas and perspectives

Passion
A commitment to engaging emotionally

Perseverance
A commitment to overcoming obstacles and enduring discomfort

Positivity
A commitment to adopting an optimistic mindset and perspective

Rationality
A commitment to making decisions based on logic and reason

Relationships
A commitment to building, maintaining, and strengthening inter-personal connections

Resilience
A commitment to overcoming setbacks and building and maintaining momentum

Respect
A commitment to treating people and things as if they have inherent value

Self-awareness
A commitment to an ongoing reflection on your thoughts, feelings, and experiences in order build a better understanding of yourself

Self-respect
A commitment to making decisions that recognize four things:

1. You have as much right to happiness as anyone else does.
2. You cannot add value to anyone else's life until you've added enough value to your own.

3. Your happiness is your responsibility
4. Happiness is not possible without forgiveness.

Service

A commitment to contributing to a collective

Tradition

A commitment to honoring the positive parts of the past

Vision

A commitment to creating and sharing idealized versions of yourself, others, organizations, and communities

Vulnerability

A commitment to being open about things that could hurt you

Sample Action-Driving Questions

Accountability
A commitment to delivering on promises and acknowledging responsibility for the outcomes of your actions

How did I honor a commitment today?
How did I own a mistake today?
What did I do today to build trust?

Adaptability
A commitment to change when necessary

How did I adjust course today?
How did I accommodate the unexpected today?
How did I roll with a punch today?

Adventure

A commitment to seeking out new and/or exciting experiences

> *What did I do today that might become a story?*
> *How did I add excitement to my life today?*
> *How did I add something new to my life today?*

Authenticity

A commitment to making decisions based on your own beliefs and values rather than the expectations of others

> *What did I do today that I might be proud of in five years?*
> *What did I do today that was undeniably "me"?*
> *How did I demonstrate something was important to me today?*

Autonomy

A commitment to seeking independence

> *How was I my own boss today?*
> *What did I do today to build self-reliance?*
> *What opportunity did I create for myself today?*

Balance

A commitment to pursuing equilibrium in your thoughts, action, and being

> *What priority did I honor today that I didn't honor yesterday?*
> *How did I make time for something important to me today?*
> *How did I add variety to my life today?*

Class

A commitment to treating people and situations better than they deserve to be treated, even when you have every right not to

How did I elevate instead of escalate today?
How did I treat someone better than they deserved to be treated today?
What did I do today to make a difficult situation better?

Collaboration

A commitment to cooperating with others in the pursuit of goals

How did I work with someone else today?
What did I do today to be a good teammate?
How did I contribute to a group goal today?

Courage

A commitment to taking action when there is a possibility of loss

What did I try today that might not have worked, but I tried it anyway?
What did I do today that scared me?
What did I do today that I wanted to avoid?

Creativity

A commitment to generating ideas and behaving in ways that are different than your norm

How did I create something new in my life today?
What possibility did I explore today?
How did I think or act differently than I normally do today?

Curiosity
A commitment to asking questions and seeking answers

When did I ask "Why?" today?
What did I try to discover today?
What did I do to seek new knowledge today?

Decisiveness
A commitment to taking definitive action

To what choice did I commit today?
How did I make a decision and move on today?
What did I do today to stick to a recent decision?

Discipline
A commitment to overcoming distractions

What excuse did I refuse to make today?
How did I honor a commitment to myself today?
What did I do today that I also did yesterday?

Drive
A commitment to creating or maintaining momentum

What new options did I generate for myself today?
What did I do today that will generate momentum?
What new goal did I set today?

Empathy

A commitment to trying to understand and share the experiences and emotions of others

> *How did I strive to better understand someone today?*
> *What did I do today to make someone feel less alone?*
> *How did I let someone know I cared even if I couldn't fully understand?*

Empowerment

A commitment to acting as a catalyst for the success of others

> *What did I do today to move someone else closer to a goal?*
> *What did I do today that I wish someone else had done for me at some point in my life?*
> *How was I a teacher today?*
> *How did I make someone stronger today?*

Fairness

A commitment to equal opportunity

> *What did I do to make the world more equitable today?*
> *What barrier to equity did I work to remove today?*
> *What did I do today to fight inequality?*

Faith

A commitment to having an absolute trust in something

> *How did I honor God today?*
> *How did I recognize that something was beyond my control today?*
> *How did I demonstrate acceptance today?*

Family

A commitment to prioritizing the relationships of those you consider family

> *What did I do today to show my family they are important to me?*
> *How did I put family first today?*
> *How did I say "I love you" without saying it?*

Forgiveness

A commitment to letting go of negative thoughts and emotions about those who have harmed you (including yourself)

> *How did I show compassion today?*
> *How did I let go of something negative today?*
> *How did I try to make peace today?*

Fun

A commitment to creating, finding, or embracing moments of enjoyment

> *How did I play today?*
> *How did I act like a kid today?*
> *How did I enjoy a moment today?*

Generosity

A commitment to identifying, seeking out, or creating opportunities to give more than is required of yourself and your resources

When did I give more than just what I "had to" today?

What did I give away today I could have easily kept for myself?

Who received something from me today I wasn't required to give?

Gratitude
A commitment to honor the good, the bad, and the ugly in your life for the person those experiences help you become

What did I do today to say "thank you"?

How did I celebrate something in my life today?

How did I let someone know I appreciate them today?

Growth
A commitment to expanding the capacity to add value

What did I do today to make it more likely someone would learn something?

What did I do today that will make me more effective tomorrow?

What did I do today to get better?

Happiness
A commitment to generating positive emotions

What did I do to make myself feel good today?

What did I do today to create a positive moment?

Which one of my favorite things did I do today?

Health

A commitment to engaging in actions that contribute to physical, psychological, emotional, spiritual, and intellectual strength and wellness

> *What did I do today to make myself stronger?*
> *What did I do today that might add even a single second to my life?*
> *How did I feed the best part of me today?*

Humility

A commitment to recognizing that the things which make you awesome don't make you better than anyone else

> *How did I reflect someone else's light today?*
> *How did I acknowledge someone else's role in my success today?*
> *How did I use my resources to make someone else look good today?*

Impact

A commitment to creating moments that cause people to feel they are better off for having interacted with you

> *How have I recognized someone else's leadership today?*
> *What conscious act of kindness did I perform today?*
> *What did I do today to show someone that they matter?*

Innovation

A commitment to challenging and improving the status quo

How did I challenge "the way it's always been done" today?
How did I try to improve a process today?
What did I do today that could contribute to a positive change?

Integrity
A commitment to using a consistent set of values for decision making

How did I reference my values today?
What did I do today that demonstrates one of my core values?
How did I recognize when I could have been better today?

Kindness
A commitment to creating moments where someone feels their well-being was your only motivation for doing something.

How did I generate a smile in someone else today?
What did I do today to make someone feel like their burdens were just a little bit lighter for a moment?
What did I do today that was entirely about making someone else feel better?

Love
A commitment to creating emotional connections without conditions

How did I open my heart today?
How did I give unconditionally today?
What did I do today to make connecting with someone easier?

Loyalty

A commitment to honoring your connections and commitments

How did I show someone I have their back today?
How did I demonstrate trust in someone today?
How did I live up to an expectation today?

Mastery

A commitment to seeking continuous improvement

How did I practice something today?
How did I invest in my craft today?
What did I do today to learn from someone better?

Mindfulness

A commitment to being conscious, aware, and engaged in any given moment

What did I do today to be truly present in a moment?
What did I do today to give the present the attention it deserves?
What did I do today to completely focus on the needs of another?

Open-mindedness

A commitment to exploring the validity of new ideas and perspectives

How did I challenge one of my beliefs today?
What did I do today to seek out a new perspective?
What did I do today to encourage someone to share their beliefs?

Passion

A commitment to engaging emotionally

What did I do today to make myself feel more alive?
How did I enthusiastically say yes today?
What did I do today to generate the feelings I love the most?

Perseverance

A commitment to overcoming obstacles and enduring discomfort

What did I overcome today?
When did I refuse to quit today?
How did I move on from a failure today?

Positivity

A commitment to adopting an optimistic mindset and perspective

When did I refuse to be negative today?
When did I ask "what could go right" today?
How did I create a "best-case scenario" today?

Rationality

A commitment to making decisions based on logic and reason

How did I play devil's advocate today?
How did I seek outside advice today?
How did I do what was right instead of what felt right?

Relationships

A commitment to building, maintaining, and strengthening interpersonal connections

What did I do today to create or strengthen a community?
How did I demonstrate to someone that they matter to me today?
What did I do today to strengthen an interpersonal connection?
How did I renew a connection with someone today?

Resilience

A commitment to overcoming setbacks and building and maintaining momentum

What did I do today to honor my commitment to be okay?
What did I do today to move forward?
What did I do today to see myself as more than my failures?

Respect

A commitment to treating people and things as if they have inherent value

What did I do today to better understand someone?
What did I do today to show someone I felt they were valuable?
How did I disagree with civility today?

Self-awareness

A commitment to an ongoing reflection on your thoughts, feelings, and experiences in order build a better understanding of yourself

How did I challenge something I believed in today?
What did I do today to learn something about myself?
How did I ask for feedback today?

Self-respect

A commitment to making decisions that recognize four things:

1. You have as much right to happiness as anyone else does.
2. You cannot add value to anyone else's life until you've added enough value to your own.
3. Your happiness is your responsibility.
4. Happiness is not possible without forgiveness.

What did I do today to be good to myself?
How was I my own best friend today?
What did I do today to prioritize my own needs?

Service

A commitment to contributing to a collective

How did I strengthen a community today?
How did I give of myself to something bigger today?

Tradition

A commitment to honoring the positive parts of the past

What did I do today to honor those who have come before me?
How did I recognize a valuable part of the past today?
What part of the past did I use to create a better future today?

Vision

A commitment to creating and sharing idealized versions of yourself, others, organizations, and communities

What did I do today to remind someone how things should be?

How did I inspire others to strive for better today?

When did I ask "what if" today?

Vulnerability

A commitment to being open about things that could hurt you

What did I choose not to hide today?

How was I open about something that scared me today?

When was I honest about a personal shortcoming today?

Value Tally Sheet

Each time one of the following values is identified as foundational for a piece of your Edge of the Bed Advice place a tally next to it. Each time one of the following values is identified as foundational for one of your moments of pride or disappointment, place two (2) tallies next to it.

Accountability	_____	Faith	_____
Adaptability	_____	Family	_____
Adventure	_____	Forgiveness	_____
Authenticity	_____	Fun	_____
Autonomy	_____	Generosity	_____
Balance	_____	Gratitude	_____
Class	_____	Growth	_____
Collaboration	_____	Happiness	_____
Courage	_____	Health	_____
Creativity	_____	Humility	_____
Curiosity	_____	Impact	_____
Decisiveness	_____	Innovation	_____
Discipline	_____	Integrity	_____
Drive	_____	Kindness	_____
Empathy	_____	Love	_____
Empowerment	_____	Loyalty	_____
Fairness	_____	Mastery	_____

Mindfulness	_____	Respect	_____
Open-mindedness	_____	Self-awareness	_____
Passion	_____	Self-respect	_____
Perseverance	_____	Service	_____
Positivity	_____	Tradition	_____
Rationality	_____	Vision	_____
Relationships	_____	Vulnerability	_____
Resilience	_____		

ACKNOWLEDGMENTS

My friend Josh told me he finds it much classier when an author lists just a few people in the acknowledgments. Sorry my friend, it's my first book and there are a lot of people to thank for making it a reality.

First, thanks to Mom, Dad, and Sarah for putting up with a career where strangers hear my voice more than you do.

From the moment I sat down with Jim Levine I knew he was the man to begin guiding me through a process I found more than a little intimidating. My sincere thanks to him and everyone at Levine Greenberg Rostan.

I often say the three most important words in leadership are "I don't know." Thanks to Mauro DiPreta, Joanna Pinsker, Michael Barrs, Odette Fleming, David Lamb, Cheryl Smith, and the entire team at Hachette Book Group for being willing to hear those three words from me so often.

When someone gives a speaker the opportunity to share ideas with their audience, they are placing their reputation in the hands of someone they have usually never met. I am honored by the trust shown me by all my clients and hosts over the years.

To the leaders featured in this book: thank you for sharing

your stories, insights, triumphs, and failures. I hope I did them justice.

When I look back to my earliest Day Ones, I must recognize Susie Wills, Craig Harris, and Barry Driscoll for being the teachers who helped me take my gaze off the double-sided sheet of paper and inspired me to aim much higher.

My earliest leadership successes were made possible by the time, support, and resources of two men in particular: Jonathan Clark and Ian Allen. Thank you, old friends.

I've seen twenty years of volunteers and staff dedicate their time and passion to *Shinerama: Students Fighting Cystic Fibrosis.* That campaign has generated more laughter and friendships than any other part of my life, and no mention of my experience there would be complete without a message of love to Tracey Adams.

Without Tom Nowers, Mark Solomon, and Amy Gaukel some of my most important professional Day Ones may never have happened. Thank you for the chances each of you took on me.

My thanks to the first group to take on the "Edge of the Bed Assignment": Lisa Zenno, Jeff Van Geel, Nogah Kornberg, Anastasia Smallwood, Chris Read, Sarah Cousineau, Ammad Khan, Stephen Fernez, Laura Reinsborough, and Faren Hochman. I am grateful for the hours you spent helping me refine one of the most important parts of the project.

When I needed answers about what questions to ask, a dream team gave up a weekend of their lives to help: Jordan Axani, Steph Berntson, Shane Feldman, Blake Fleischacker, Hamza Khan, Bailey Parnell, Arjune Selvarajan, and Brigitte

Truong. Many hands make light work, but many minds make great work. Thank you all.

I don't think Chad Randall, Mary Rupert, Alex Boyce-Vienneau, and my entire 9Round family are truly aware how big a role they played in bringing me back to life. I wouldn't have made it through the final stretch without you.

A framed napkin bearing the words "This Is Day One" sat next to my keyboard through the toughest part of this process, a constant reminder of how blessed I am to have earned the friendship and forgiveness of a small group of extraordinary people. Through the first steps, next steps, wrong steps, and new steps they have remained: Mike Allison, Josh Bragg, Marc Carnes, Kelly Francis, Allan Grant, Christy Holtby, Pam Hrick, Adam Langer, and Jess Patterson. Thank you for the gift Danielle, that was awfully nice of you.

Finally, Sasha: there are no words to describe what your strength and friendship mean to me.

Look around, look around at how lucky we are to be alive right now.

ENDNOTES

1. J. Kouzes and B. Posner, (2017). *The Leadership Challenge*, 8th ed. (Hoboken, NJ: John Wiley & Sons, 2017) 128.
2. B. Zeigarnik, (1927). Über das Behalten von erledigten und uneredigten Handlungen. *Psychologische Forschung*, 9: 1–85.
3. Sarah Wilding, Mark Conner, Tracy Sandberg, Andrew Prestwich, Rebecca Lawton, Chantelle Wood, Eleanor Miles, Gaston Godin, & Paschal Sheeran (2016). The question-behaviour effect: A theoretical and methodological review and meta-analysis. *European Review of Social Psychology*, 27:1, 196–230, DOI: 10.1080/10463283.2016. 1245940.
4. Inspired by Comely, entrepreneur Jia Jiang chronicled 100 days of rejection in his 2015 book *Rejection Proof*. In 2017, Jiang's TED Talk "What I Learned from 100 Days of Rejection" became one of the year's most popular talks. You can find out more at rejection therapy.com.
5. For a fascinating exploration of how human evolution and emotion impact leadership, read Daniel Goleman's brilliant book *Primal Leadership*.
6. Though I define it slightly differently, I was first exposed to this term through Wolfgang Hoeschele's book *The Economics of Abundance: A Political Economy of Freedom, Equity, and Sustainability*.
7. The man in question is Dr. James Maskalyk, author of *Six Months in Sudan: A Young Doctor in a War-Torn Village*.
8. J. Kouzes and B. Posner, (2017). *The Leadership Challenge*, 8th ed. (Hoboken, NJ: John Wiley & Sons, 2017) 147.